THE BASIS OF DURABLE PEACE

THE BASIS
OF DURABLE PEACE

WRITTEN AT THE INVITATION
OF THE
NEW YORK TIMES

BY

COSMOS

NEW YORK
CHARLES SCRIBNER'S SONS
1917

PUBLISHER'S NOTE

These papers were originally printed in
The New York Times of November 20,
21, 22, 23, 24, 25, 27, 28, 30, and December 2, 4, 6, 9, 12, 15, and 18, 1916.

INTRODUCTION

PEACE AND ITS CONDITIONS

RECENT utterances of the German Chancellor and the British Prime Minister have inclined the discerning public to the belief that the chief men of the warring nations in Europe would now give more hospitable consideration than they have shown in the past to proposals embodying the broad general principles upon which peace must be concluded. Sharing that belief, *The New York Times* invited, from a source the competence and authority of which would be recognized in both hemispheres, a series of contributions in which the terms of peace should be discussed.

As the publication of the series proceeded from day to day the public perceived the candor, the impartial fairness, the breadth of view, and the profound understanding of political principles with which the author weighed and considered the general conditions of peace, and then in turn the policies and interests of each of the Powers engaged in the war. All of them profess a desire for peace upon terms that will insure its permanency. In these discussions the way to lasting peace is brought into view, the rivalry of ambition and the clash of in-

terests are so far as may be conciliated, and a settlement compatible with the demands of justice,
with the rights of small and great nations, and giving promise of freedom from the calamity of war is
submitted to the public judgment.

The New York Times has confidence that the public here and abroad will give serious attention to
these papers because of the breadth of knowledge and
far-seeing statesmanship they display, quite independent of the distinguished source from which they
come.

December, 1916.

CONTENTS

I

CONTENTS

CONTENTS

XIV

XV

XVI

THE BASIS OF DURABLE PEACE

I

IS THE END OF THE WAR IN SIGHT?——RECENT BRIT-
ISH AND GERMAN STATEMENTS AS TO THE AIMS
OF THE WAR——THEIR SIMILARITY IN FORM

THE time has come to consider whether the
war may not shortly be ended by international agreement in which the United States
shall participate.

For some months past the centre of gravity of the
world's interest has been steadily shifting. It is now
coming to rest at a new and gravely significant spot.
The question as to who or what power is chiefly
responsible for the last events that immediately
preceded the war has become for the moment one
of merely historical interest. It may not be settled
to the universal satisfaction for a generation to
come. The importance of the war's issues has
thrust into the background the discussion of the
war's direct causes. The amazing records of the
war's progress, with their alternate pages of cruelty
and of heroism, of devastation and of self-sacrifice, of
carnage and of superb national achievement, are so
many and so crowded that they have overtaxed
human appreciation and human understanding.
We are now left unwillingly dull and insensitive
to happenings almost any one of which would or-
dinarily stir the imagination and inspire the art and
the letters of a civilized world.

Men everywhere were so appalled by the magnitude of the war when it suddenly broke out, and so amazed at its revelations and its massive consequences in life, in treasure, and in sacrifice, that for more than two years they could see no solution of the world-wide problem that it raised other than to permit the war to run its course until one of the groups of great adversaries was forced to succumb. It was freely predicted that this end would be reached in three months, in six months, or at most in a year. Almost alone, Lord Kitchener indicated three years as the probable duration of the war. Of that period nearly two and a half years have already passed, and no end is in sight. Nevertheless, some things are now plain to the watching world. It is clear that the German Empire and its allies cannot win this war. That fact, which was confident prophecy after the battle of the Marne and reasonable expectation after the failure at Verdun and the happenings along the eastern front, has been made certain by the battle of the Somme, already drawn out over four long months, and by Great Britain's unbroken, complete command of the seas. It is also clear that, while Great Britain and her allies can, and doubtless will, win the war, yet the cost will be so unbelievably great and the resulting exhaustion in men, in money, and in industry, so alarming, that victory on such terms can be only little less disastrous than defeat.

Both in the warring countries and in neutral lands there has been of late much discussion as to how similar outbreaks of international war may be avoided in the future. This is certainly a highly practical question for governments and for peoples. But a still more practical question for governments and for peoples is how to bring this present war to an end without waiting for more complete exhaustion, more and more wide-spread destruction, and more and more far-reaching damage to civilization —provided always that the great issues of moral principle that are at stake be rightly decided.

There are not lacking signs that the belligerent powers are ready to have this question pressed upon them with directness and with vigor. To undertake this means, first of all, to try to find a common ground for discussion. In order to do that we must go to the belligerent nations for a statement of what they severally conceive to be the objects for which the war is now continued. This, in turn, means that we must go first to Great Britain and to Germany for an answer.

The war began ostensibly as a conflict between Austria-Hungary on the one side and Serbia on the other. With lightning-like rapidity the fact developed that this conflict in the southeastern corner of Europe was not a cause but a symptom, and that the materials for a world war lay ready to hand in the ambitions, suspicions, rivalries, and world policies of the great powers to the north and west. It is increasingly clear that the war is, in last analysis, really a titanic struggle between two sharply contrasted views of government and of life with Germany and Great Britain as protagonists. The first attack on Serbia was to strengthen the position and to advance the policies of the Central Powers. The springing to arms of Russia was to prevent the further subjection of a Slavic people. The quick arming of Germany was to ward off a possible attack from the east, on the one hand, and, now that the fire had been lighted, to push forward to gain control of the seas on the other. The invasion of Belgium was not an end, but a means. The invasion and threatened conquest of France was not an end, but a means. The end was Calais, the Straits of Dover, Great Britain, and the control of the seven seas. All this we can now see.

How does the matter stand to-day? Are these once obvious ends still controlling the minds and the policies of the warring peoples? Death, suffering, and privation have given to the word WAR a new and terrible meaning for peoples who had known a long generation of peace. While in no belligerent country is there any weakening of effort or lack of conviction of the justness of their cause, there are everywhere the plain beginnings of an effort to seek some solution of the war's problems that will not mean the continuance, perhaps for a decade, of the present reign of bloodshed and destruction. The air is filled with wireless messages from chiefs of state. Who is to catch them, to interpret them, to act upon them? It is contrary to the etiquette of war for Great Britain just now to speak to Germany, or for Germany to make polite reply to Great

Britain. But when Mr. Asquith and Viscount Grey speak in Parliament on the ends and objects of the war, to whom are they really addressing themselves? When the Imperial German Chancellor rises before the Reichstag and makes reply to published statements of Viscount Grey, to whom is he addressing himself? Is it not the fact that these statesmen are at this very moment really discussing publicly terms of peace and the conditions on which this war may be ended, while seeming only to make formal statements to their immediate colleagues?

Speaking to the Foreign Press Association in London on October 23, Viscount Grey used these words:

> I take it on the word of the Prime Minister that we shall fight until we have established *the supremacy and right of free development under equal conditions, each in accordance with its genius, of all States, great and small, as a family of civilized mankind.*

That is a noble ideal, which must waken response in every liberty-loving breast throughout the world, and one must applaud Viscount Grey's assurance that "when we are asked how long the struggle is to continue, we can only reply that it must continue until these things are secured." But is it a fact that these ends can be secured only by continuing this struggle to its desperate finish?

It so happens that we are not left in doubt as to Germany's answer. On November 9 Chancellor von Bethmann-Hollweg, speaking to what is called the main committee of the Reichstag, made specific reference to this statement by Viscount Grey. He insisted, of course, that the war was forced upon Germany, and that as a consequence Germany would be entitled to ask for guarantees against similar attacks in the future. But he added much the most significant statement that has been made in German official life in the memory of any man now living. These are his momentous words:

> We never concealed our doubts that peace could be guaranteed permanently by international organizations such as arbitration courts. I shall not discuss the theoretical aspects of the problem in this place. But from the standpoint of matters of fact we now and in time of peace must define our position with regard to this question.
>
> If at and after the end of the war the world will only become fully conscious of the horrifying destruction of life and property, then through the whole of humanity there will ring out a cry for peaceful arrangements and understandings which, as far as they are within human power, will prevent the return of such a monstrous catastrophe. This cry will be so powerful and so justified that it must lead to some result.
>
> *Germany will honestly co-operate in the examination of every endeavor to find a practical solution, and will collaborate for its possible realization.* This all the more if the war, as we expect and trust, brings about political conditions that do full justice to *the free development of all nations, of small as well as great nations.* Then the principles of justice and free development, not only on the Continent but also on the seas, must be made valid. This, to be sure, Viscount Grey did not mention.

A comparison of these two profoundly important declarations indicates that it ought not to be impossible to find a formula as to the free development of all States, great and small, as members of a single family of nations, that would satisfy both the British Foreign Secretary and the Imperial German Chancellor.

Two questions immediately present themselves. When Viscount Grey and Chancellor von Bethmann-Hollweg use substantially the same words as to the free development of all nations, do they really mean the same thing? If so, how are we to explain Belgium and Serbia? And then what about the conditions on the seas?

II

WHEN Viscount Grey and Chancellor von
Bethmann-Hollweg use substantially the
same words in regard to establishing the
right of all nations, great and small, to free development, do they really mean the same thing?

History will prove a more useful guide to an
answer than merely theoretical discussion. The
record of Great Britain, particularly that part of
the record which has been made by the Liberal
Governments of the last seventy-five years, is
enviable, with a single exception. Russell, Palmerston, Gladstone, Campbell-Bannerman, and Asquith have consistently given support to weak and
struggling nationalities aiming for greater freedom,
as well as sympathy to those nationalities that
were submerged under conquering nations. Great
Britain befriended Belgium and Italy and Greece.
In Canada, in Australia, and in South Africa she
has pursued a colonial policy as wise as it has been
able. The much-denounced actions of Mr. Gladstone after Majuba Hill and of Sir Henry Campbell-Bannerman after the South African war re-

sulted in binding the South African people more
closely than ever before to the British Empire.
The one weakness in Great Britain's dealing with
the problem of nationality is found in Ireland.
The Irish question, complicated as it has been by
problems of land ownership, of violent religious
antipathy, and of traditional race antagonism,
appeared to be well on the way to at least a pro-
visional solution when the war broke out, and
perhaps even greater progress may be made so
soon as the war shall end.

Since 1846 the free trade policy of Great Britain
has undoubtedly been of great advantage to the
world at large and to every nation whether great
or small. If it could speedily have become universal, to-day's problems of international trade
and commerce would be wholly different, and some
at least of the causes of international war would
have been removed. Great Britain has not only
supported the policy of the open door abroad, but
she alone among the greater nations has kept an
open door at home. The sharp differences of opinion that have arisen among the British people
themselves during the past twenty years as to
the success of the free trade policy, when measured
by its effects at home, are not relevant to this discussion. What concerns the world at large is the
obvious fact that this free trade policy has been a
benefit to every other nation, whether great or
small. It has offered them the stimulus of a British
market and the added stimulus of British com-

petition. The history of German trade proves that Germany has everything to gain and nothing to lose by Great Britain's policy.

Therefore, it is only fair to infer in view of these facts that Viscount Grey means that every nation, whether great or small, should be at liberty to develop as Belgium, as Italy, and as Greece have developed; that to every dependent nationality there should be granted that full measure of self-government which is characteristic of Canada, of Australia, and of South Africa; and that international trade should be as little restricted and hampered as possible. This policy would satisfy liberal-minded men everywhere and would put international peace on a more secure foundation than it has ever had before.

The record of the dealings of Germany with other nations, particularly small nations, is a different one. This difference is due, no doubt, in part to different circumstances from those which have confronted Great Britain. It is, however, due in part to a distinct public policy. Germany, unlike Great Britain, has not found itself in island seclusion, but with long and easily crossed frontiers that marched with those of other and quite different peoples. The relation of Germany to Poland and to Denmark has been somewhat the same as that in which England stood to Scotland and to Wales in the time of the three Edwards. In the latter case the resulting wars ended, however, in a really united Great Britain, and not in submerged and unhappy subject populations. At this moment the Prime Minister of England sits for a Scottish constituency and the Minister for War is a Welshman. Germany's treatment of Poland, of the Schleswig-Holstein duchies, and of Alsace-Lorraine has been unfortunate, to say the least, from the standpoint of a nation which is concerned for the free development of all nations, whether great or small. The plea of national necessity urged in explanation of this treatment, as in defense of the invasion of Belgium, is not convincing to modern ears. Yet it must not be too lightly set aside through lack of capacity to see the German point of view.

Prince von Bülow has described the policy of Germany toward Poland as a "mission of civilization," and he says that, if Prussia had not taken possession of that part of Poland which now constitutes the Eastern Provinces, these provinces would have fallen under the dominion of Russia. In this statement there are two implications. The first is that it would be disadvantageous to the national development of Germany if these provinces had fallen into the hands of Russia. The second is that Germany could make better provision for the development of Poland, or for that part of it which was annexed, than Poland could make for itself. The first of these implications opens the door to a long debate which, in view of the established facts, would now be futile. The second raises a definite question which bears directly upon the meaning of the words, "the right of all nations, great and small, to free development." If Poland, being a nation, possessing a language, a literature, and a body of traditions of its own, does not itself wish to be submerged under either Germany or Russia, then so to submerge it would appear to be in violation of the principles which Chancellor von Bethmann-Hollweg now announces as his own. The Allies are publicly committed to an autonomous Poland. A solution might perhaps be found if the Chancellor's language were interpreted to mean that, in such cases as those of the Poles and the South Slavs, the peoples in question should be given an opportunity to decide for themselves whether they prefer autonomy with national independence or autonomy with dependence on a greater and neighboring Power. In order to satisfy the liberal opinion of the world, such peoples, and those of Ireland as well, must have autonomy. National independence, where it has long been lost or where it has never been gained, raises another set of questions which can hardly be answered save after detailed examination of each particular case.

Therefore, whether Chancellor von Bethmann-Hollweg and Viscount Grey are in agreement upon this point would seem to turn upon whether Germany is willing to permit the Poles and the South Slavs to choose the form of their own political organization and to direct it when organized. If so, agreement between Germany and Great Britain, in this respect at least, is certainly in sight. Should Germany demur on the ground that her own national security is at stake, the answer must be found in those new forms of international guarantee for national security which it is hoped will be proposed and adopted at the end of the war.

More than once in the past it has been the policy of Germany to acquire, when possible, exclusive trade privileges and to insist upon them. Germany has not had the opportunity which the sixteenth, seventeenth, and eighteenth centuries brought to England, of establishing great colonial dependencies in the temperate zone, and therefore she has not been tested as England has been by the government of a Canada, or an Australia, or a South Africa. Yet, as far as the record goes, it indicates that Germany appears to favor exclusive trade privileges, if only as a basis for diplomatic negotiations, while England supports the open door. It must therefore be considered what advantage there would be in any proposal that would bring Germany to the support of an open door policy as a means of binding the nations of the world more closely together and of removing one great cause of international rivalry and jealousy.

III

THE OPEN DOOR IN INTERNATIONAL TRADE AS AN
INFLUENCE FOR PEACE—ECONOMIC WAR AND
PRIVILEGE A CERTAIN CAUSE OF INTERNA-
TIONAL UNREST

WHAT may, for convenience, be called the
open door policy of international trade
does not necessarily imply the total aban-
donment of tariffs, either for revenue or indeed for
protection, if that which is to be protected is in each
case conceived as a really human and not merely a
money interest. In so far as tariffs are levied by
any nation as a necessary means of raising revenue,
or in so far as they are, in the judgment of any nation, necessary to the protection of the standard
of living of wage-earners or to the diversification of
industry, and in so far as they apply equally to all
nations, they are compatible with the open door
policy in the broad sense. What the open door
policy does involve is a changed point of view on
the part of those nations which like Germany,
France, and the United States, have been too
largely under the domination of the notion that all
imports are harmful, and that they displace an equal
amount of home-made products. So long as any one
great nation holds to the false theory that international trade is a mere casual incident to a nation's

business, and sometimes even a detriment to it, just so long will other great nations hold aloof and keep their excluding tariff walls more or less in repair. Whatever is done to make international trade more easy and more general must be done by the common consent of the great commercial nations of the world.

There can be little doubt that false and misleading views of international trade have had more to do with the development of those international rivalries and suspicions which preceded and made possible the present war than any other single cause. How to remove these rivalries and suspicions, and how to substitute a new, a wiser, and a broader view of international trade for that which has heretofore prevailed, is one of the most serious aspects of the problem of effecting a genuine peace.

This question cannot be settled by economists alone. Indeed, they are incompetent to settle it, as is made clear enough by the fact that the three most prominent German economists in this generation have held sharply differing views on this question. Professor Wagner has taught thoroughgoing protection, Professor Brentano has taught complete free trade, while Professor Schmoller has taken a middle course. Similar divisions, though perhaps not always quite so definite as these, have existed in the ranks of French, British, Italian, Russian, and American economists. This question is to be settled, if at all, on the broad basis of constructive statesmanship and from the view-point of a just and secure international peace to which each nation must be willing to make its contribution.

The fact must not be overlooked that there is in Great Britain a powerful body of political opinion, strongly supported by some economists, which would reverse the British trade policy of the past sixty years and institute a régime of new trade antagonism and new international suspicion. It would be little short of calamitous should the trade policy of Great Britain be essentially changed now. The swift concurrence of other nations in a liberal trade policy, which Cobden and Bright foresaw and so confidently predicted a half century ago, did not result, but there never has been so favorable a chance for the concurrence of other nations as now presents itself. The pressure of the universal desire for a stable peace may accomplish what generations of argument and example could not do. If Great Britain will only persist in her present trade policy she may thereby make an even greater contribution to the peace of the world than she can possibly make by her navy, her army, and her almost limitless financial resources.

The Economic Conference of the Allied Powers, held in Paris on June 14–17, 1916, was most significant. To the extent to which the conference dealt with economic measures to be taken by them during the war, its conclusions and recommendations need not be discussed here. In so far, however, as this conference foreshadowed a period of purposeful and highly organized economic strife after the present military struggle is ended, it was discouraging and reactionary in the extreme. Two generations ago Lord Clarendon, in referring to the apparent settlement of the Eastern question by the Treaty of Paris, wrote: "Nous avons fait *une* paix, mais pas *la* paix." If the present military contest is to be immediately succeeded by a new and vigorous economic struggle, using all the implements of privilege, discrimination, and favor, then while the war may result in *a* peace, it will not result in that durable and secure peace on which the heart of the world is set.

Meanwhile the people of the United States, at least, are at school. The war has literally forced upon them an international trade of stupendous magnitude, and it is rapidly transforming them from a debtor into a creditor nation. Since the outbreak of the war the people of the United States have bought back from Europe considerably more than $2,000,000,000 of their own securities, and, in addition, they have loaned nearly, if not quite, $2,000,-000,000 to foreign countries and municipalities. These new and highly profitable experiences, taken in connection with the fact that for some years past American public opinion has been gradually taking larger and sounder views of international trade and of tariff problems, indicate that in the United States the ruling tendency is in the right direction. Such facts teach the American people, more thoroughly than any printed page can possibly do, what it means to engage in international trade on so huge a scale, and how it broadens the sympathies and widens the knowledge of all those who, directly or indirectly, are interested in the undertaking. " For where your treasure is, there will your heart be also."

The Allies have an unexampled opportunity to lay the foundations of a durable peace if, when the war ends, they will offer to Germany and her allies complete participation on equal terms in the trade of the world, on the sole condition that political activity in other countries be abandoned and that an international guarantee for national security be at once agreed upon. Neither the Allies nor Germany need fear that in such case the influence of their national ideals, their public policies, or their literatures will be lost. It is undeniable, as the late Professor William G. Sumner once wrote, that: "We may be very sure that the wheat from America has had far more effect on ideas in Europe than the ideas from America."

IV

IN application of the principles thus far discussed it would appear that agreement between Great Britain and Germany in regard to establishing "the right of all nations, great and small, to free development" probably depends upon the granting of autonomy to Ireland, to Poland, and to the South Slavonic peoples, as well as upon the general adoption of the open door policy in foreign trade. Belgium must, of course, be restored and indemnified by Germany. In like manner Serbia must be restored and indemnified by Austria-Hungary. Underlying and supporting all of these acts would be a new international guarantee for the national security of all peoples, great and small alike. If the mind of Great Britain and the mind of Germany could meet on these points—and why should they not?—there is no reason to suppose that either France or Russia would hold back, unless perhaps it might be in regard to the more complete application of the open door policy in foreign trade. But France, who seeks nothing unreasonable for herself, and asks only national security and the protection of the principles of public conduct in which she ar-

dently believes, would almost certainly assent to
a plan that would ask her to sacrifice so little in
the way of a modified economic policy in order to
attain so much of permanent good for herself and
for the world.   The situation as regards Russia
appears to be quite similar, particularly if Russia
can be assured of that free access to the sea throughout the year which she has so long desired, and
which she should have in the general interest as
well as in her own.

There would then remain the one important
question referred to by Chancellor von Bethmann-
Hollweg in his speech of November 9 last, and not
mentioned by Viscount Grey in his speech of October
23, namely, the conditions on the seas.

That Germany is deeply concerned on this point
has long been apparent.   The freedom of the seas
is one of the five points covered by the peace programme of the Bund Neues Vaterland.   It is made
one of the peace aims of the German Socialists.
Doctor Dernburg includes it in his six proposals
for peace made public on April 18, 1915.   The Imperial German Chancellor evidently lays great
stress upon it.   One must inquire, therefore, just
what is meant by the freedom of the seas and in
what respect that freedom is now lacking or denied.

Under existing international law the seas are,
and long have been, free outside of the conventional
three-mile limit.   There are no longer any pirates,
and no charge is made for traversing the seas between one port and another.   There are no rights

of way over the ocean. In law, therefore, the seas would seem to be even freer than the land. Small peoples with insignificant navies, such as the Norwegians, the Danes, the Dutch, and the Portuguese, have been and are successful sea traders to no inconsiderable extent. Germany herself has, within the past forty years, built up a stupendous merchant marine, and at the outbreak of the present war her flag was as familiar as any other in the seaports of six continents. It would appear, then, that the desired freedom of the seas has nothing to do with the normal conditions of international peace; it must relate entirely to the abnormal conditions of international war. So far, therefore, as future international wars can be guarded against and averted by an agreement upon such policies as have already been described, all differences as to freedom of the seas will disappear. If, however, the world is to contemplate another international war like that now raging, what is the ground for that German uneasiness as to the freedom of the seas which is so apparent?

It is, however, not yet entirely clear just what specific things Germany aims at in pressing for freedom of the seas. The freedom of the seas to which the United States, for example, owes its existence and its prosperity, and for which both Holland and Great Britain stoutly contended in days gone by, is the freedom which Grotius defined when he laid it down as a specific and unimpeachable axiom of the law of nations, the spirit of which

is self-evident and immutable, that: "Every nation is free to travel to every other nation, and to
trade with it." It is in this broad and fundamental
sense that the world already possesses freedom of
the seas. Those municipal regulations which so
often restrict and harass international trade have
no application on the sea itself, but only at the
ports of entry. Doubtless, however, the mind of
Germany, like the mind of Great Britain, has come
very largely under the dominance of the argument
of that American book which, on the whole, has
had more influence in shaping modern European
policy than any other work published on this side
of the Atlantic. That book is the late Admiral
Mahan's "Influence of Sea Power upon History."
This illuminating book has, however, nothing whatever to do with the freedom of the seas. It deals
wholly with questions relating to the control of
the seas, a quite different matter. Two of Admiral
Mahan's ruling contentions are that commerce
needs navies for its protection and that sea power
has throughout the history of war been an important and often a decisive factor. It is plain
that in time of war, and as one of the incidents of
war, the control of the seas will rest with the most
powerful and best distributed navy. At such a
time the seas cannot possibly be free to ships of
war, which must take their chances in battle with
an antagonist. What Germany doubtless has in
mind is the fact that the British Navy is not only
powerful enough to control the seas in time of war,

but that this control may be, and in the German
view is, so used as to deprive Germany and her
allies of some advantages through trade with neu-
trals to which they are legally entitled.   This nar-
rows the question down to neutral trade in time of
war, and to the exemption of private property
from capture at sea.   On this topic there has been
much discussion in recent years and the policies
to which the United States is committed have
been stated over and over again.   What, if any,
just ground of complaint against Great Britain
and her allies have Germany and the neutral nations because of the way in which Great Britain
has exercised its power of sea control in time of
war, and how far must these grievances be taken
into account in laying the foundations for a just
and stable peace?

V

IT would appear, from what has gone before, that in time of peace freedom of the seas exists in the fullest sense of the words. The disputed questions relate entirely to the status and treatment of merchant vessels and their cargoes in time of war. These questions involve the detailed consideration of blockade in time of war, of contraband of war, of unneutral service, of destruction of neutral prizes, of transfer to a neutral flag, of the enemy character of a vessel or its cargo, of convoy, of resistance to search, and of compensation. Important and delicate as all these matters are, and seriously as they have engaged the attention of naval commanders and of international lawyers, they are really all subordinate to a larger question, namely, that of the exemption of all private property at sea, not contraband of war, from capture or destruction by belligerents. Were such exemption agreed to as a ruling principle, all of the other matters mentioned would fall into place and be disposed of as parts or applications of this main principle.

The first inquiry addressed by the Government of

the United States to the Government of Great Britain after the outbreak of the present war was as to whether the British Government was willing to agree that the laws of naval warfare as laid down by the Declaration of London of 1909, should be applicable to naval warfare during the present conflict in Europe, provided that the Governments with which Great Britain was or might be at war would also agree to such application. On August 20, 1914, an Order in Council was issued directing the adoption and enforcement during the present hostilities of the convention known as the Declaration of London subject to additions and modifications. The subsequent history of the matter, including action taken by the British Government by way of addition to this Order in Council or by way of modification of it, is common knowledge. Since August, 1914, the United States has addressed formal notes to Great Britain on the subjects of contraband of war, on restraints of commerce, and in particular on the case of the American steamer *Wilhelmina*. The Government of the United States has shown itself alert to the significance of these questions and incidents of war for all neutral Powers.

On the vital point of exempting all private property at sea, not contraband of war, from capture or destruction by belligerents, the United States has taken a single and a consistent position throughout the entire history of the Government. Indeed a provision for this exemption was made part of the Treaty of Amity and Commerce of 1785 with Prussia. It was there agreed that free vessels make free goods. The signers of this treaty on behalf of the United States were Benjamin Franklin, Thomas Jefferson, and John Adams. In 1856 the United States urged the addition of this provision to the clause of the Declaration of Paris relating to privateering. The fact that such addition was refused by the other high contracting Powers led the Government of the United States to decline to adhere to the Declaration of Paris.

The formal instructions to the American delegates to the first Hague Conference, held in 1899, signed by John Hay as Secretary of State, concluded with these words:

As the United States has for many years advocated the exemption of all private property not contraband of war from hostile treatment, you are authorized to propose to the Conference the principle of extending to strictly private property at sea the immunity from destruction or capture by belligerent Powers which such property already enjoys on land as worthy of being incorporated in the permanent law of civilized nations.

Following messages on this subject from President McKinley in December, 1898, and from President Roosevelt in December, 1903, the Congress of the United States adopted on April 28, 1904, a joint resolution in the following terms:

That it is the sense of the Congress of the United States that it is desirable in the interests of uniformity of action by the maritime states in time of war that the President endeavor to bring about an understanding among the principal maritime Powers with a view to incorporating into the permanent law of civilized nations the principle of the exemption of all private property at sea, not contraband of war, from capture or destruction by belligerents.

The formal instructions to the American delegates to the second Hague Conference, held in 1907, signed by Elihu Root, then Secretary of State, contained this passage:

You will maintain the traditional policy of the United States regarding the immunity of private property of belligerents at sea.

Secretary Root then went on to discuss at some length the importance of this policy.

At the first Hague Conference the representatives of nearly all the great Powers insisted that the action of the Conference should be strictly limited to the matters specified in the Russian circular of December 30, 1898, proposing the programme of the Conference. For this reason the members of the Conference at first refused to receive any proposal from the American delegates dealing with the subject of the immunity of private property not contraband from seizure on the seas in time of war. Eventually, however, a memorial from the American delegates, which stated fully the historical and actual relation of the United States to the whole subject, was received, referred to a committee, and finally brought by that committee before the Conference. The Conference of 1899 adopted a motion referring the subject to a future Conference, so that all the American delegates were able to accomplish at that time was to keep the subject before the world for discussion.

At the second Hague Conference, which met on June 15, 1907, the subject of the private property of belligerents at sea was included in the official programme. It was among the topics referred to the Fourth Commission of the Conference, of which the chairman was M. de Martens, of Russia. A specific proposition, submitted on behalf of the United States, was supported by Brazil, Norway, Sweden, Austria-Hungary, and China. Germany, supported by Portugal, while admitting that it leaned toward the proposed inviolability of private property, made the reservation that its adoption of this principle depended upon a preliminary understanding on matters relating to contraband of war and blockade. Russia did not think the question ripe for practical solution; while Argentina declared itself categorically in favor of the continuance of the right of capture. France was ready to support the American proposal if a unanimous agreement could be reached. The representatives of Great Britain held that it was impossible to separate the question of the immunity of private property from that of commercial blockade, and that the interruption of commerce was less cruel than the massacres caused by war. Nevertheless, the British delegates declared that their Government would be ready to consider the conclusion of an agreement contemplating the abolition of the right of capture if such an agreement would further the reduction of armaments.

The proposition of the United States, when first put to a vote, obtained from the forty-four States represented 21 yeas, 11 nays, 1 abstention, and 11 States not answering. The twenty-one States voting yea included, with the United States, the following present belligerent Powers: Germany (with the reservation already referred to), Austria-Hungary, Belgium, Bulgaria, Italy, Rumania, and Turkey. Of the present belligerents France, Great Britain, Japan, Montenegro, Portugal, and Russia voted in the negative.

The discussions in the Fourth Commission give more ground than does the actual vote for believing that the proposal of the United States may be accepted at the close of the war. The expressed objections of France and Russia should now be readily overcome. The reservations made by Germany will, in the nature of things, be discussed and disposed of immediately upon the conclusion of present hostilities. There remains Great Britain, among whose people a large body of commercial opinion is already strongly in favor of the exemption of private property at sea. Only three years before the outbreak of war, at a meeting of the Council of the London Chamber of Commerce, a resolution moved by no less important a person than the late Lord Avebury, "that in the opinion of this chamber private property at sea should be declared free of capture and seizure," was carefully discussed and then adopted by a unanimous vote. Other important commercial bodies in Great Britain took similar action about the same time. The obstacle in the way to British concurrence is said to be official admiralty opinion; but this is a case in which the admiralties of the world must surely be compelled to give way to the reasonable demands of those whose property is subjected to loss and damage by persistence in the present unhappy and uncivilized policy. The whole policy of commerce destruction is really obsolete and at variance with modern notions of public and private right.

At the conclusion of hostilities this question should be pressed to a final and favorable disposition. When this is done the freedom of the seas in time of war will be as fully established as war conditions themselves will permit. Subordinate questions as to contraband and blockade and as to the specific treatment of straits and canals, ought not to be difficult to settle if, as every belligerent professes, the ruling desire is for the establishment of a permanent peace.

The importance of the freedom and safety of the ocean pathways was impressively stated by Sir Robert Laird Borden, Premier of Canada, in a speech delivered on November 18 in New York. Sir Robert Borden stated that the lesson of the war was twofold: "First, that the liberty, the security, and the free existence of our empire are dependent upon the safety of the ocean pathways, whether in peace or war; next, that while sea power cannot of itself be the instrument of world domination, it is nevertheless the most powerful instrument by which world domination can be effectually resisted. Three hundred years ago it forever crushed arrogant pretensions then brought forward to control western trade routes and to exclude therefrom the free nations of the world. Little more than a century ago it maintained freedom against world domination by a single military system. To-day it remains the shield of the same freedom, and it will so continue. This burden of so tremendous a responsibility must not rest upon Britain alone, but upon the greater commonwealth which comprises all the King's dominions."

Would it not be even better and would not Great Britain be still more secure if this burden were borne by the great commercial nations of the world linked together for the purpose of securing the freedom of the seas as an instrument and incident of a durable peace?

The common sense of mankind, however, will not be satisfied with any definition of freedom of the seas in time of war which does not frankly put in the category of murder such amazing barbarities as history will recall whenever the words *Lusitania* and *Sussex* are mentioned.

VI

IF it be assumed that Great Britain and Germany, together with their several allies, could come to an agreement as to the specific applications of the principle that every nation has a right to free development and that there should be freedom of the seas in the sense heretofore described, what conditions of a durable peace would remain to be considered?

This war has made France the hero of the nations. Whether she be judged by military prowess or by power of national organization and national self-control, the French Republic has so revealed itself as to excite the unstinted admiration and to call forth the unbounded affection of the world at large. The evidence clearly proves that France was in no respect an aggressor in the present war. She herself was promptly attacked, in part because she was the ally of Russia, in part because she was on good terms with England, and in part because the plans of the German General Staff required that the French Army be broken up and destroyed first of all. That France was unprepared for war, and, therefore, was not contemplating war, has

been obvious to every one since August 1, 1914.
For one full year her devoted armies were called
upon to hold back the great host of invaders with
only partial equipment and without a large part
of the necessary instruments of successful modern
war. The military genius of General Joffre and his
colleagues, together with the heroic bravery of the
army itself, performed a veritable miracle at the
battle of the Marne, and they have been perform-
ing a succession of miracles from that day to this.
As a fighting force the French Army has gained
new laurels, and behind the army stands the French
people, calm, confident, and clear-sighted as to the
ends for which the nation is maintaining and prosecuting its defense.

Every serious-minded and responsible French-
man intends, if it be humanly possible, to make
this the last war. The inspiration of that hope
leads the French fathers and mothers to bear with
an exalted resignation the loss of their sons. It is
the inspiration of this hope which calls out the
limitless sacrifice of women and the effort even of
the aged and the infirm.

France seeks three things as the result of this
last of wars. These have been defined by one of
her representative public men as restitution, reparation, and national security. President Poincaré,
in his address on July 14, 1916, when the war had
been nearly two years in progress, stated the French
aims a little more fully. Reviewing the sufferings
and sorrows of France, he insisted in eloquent

words that these would never weaken the nation's will. He reasserted the nation's horror of war and its passionate devotion to those policies which would prevent any return of the conditions that now prevailed, and he then defined the essentials of that just and permanent peace for which France longs and which it is determined to gain. These conditions were, first, the complete restitution of invaded French territory, whether this territory had been invaded just now or forty-six years ago; second, reparation for violations of law and for injuries done to citizens of France or its allies; and, third, such guarantees as might be necessary definitely to safeguard the national independence in the future. M. Briand, President of the Council, has more than once reiterated these views. They may, therefore, be taken as an official statement of the terms on which, and on which alone, France will make peace.

Are these terms unreasonable, and is France justified in the eyes of the world in continuing to the bitter end the struggle to secure them?

It will be simplest to examine these three proposed conditions in reverse order to that in which they are stated by President Poincaré.

The guarantees for the future to which the President refers are the crux of the whole matter. Several times in these discussions reference has been made to an international guarantee of national security in the future, and in due time the question will be raised as to how this international guarantee may be secured and in what it should consist. France is certainly entitled to the protection of this guarantee. It can and should be the same guarantee that will protect Belgium, Serbia, a reconstituted Poland, or any other small nation, as well as Great Britain, Italy, or Germany itself. In this respect, then, the demand of France is one that should and must be fairly met.

Then France demands reparation for violations of law and for damage done to her citizens and their private property, as well as to those of her allies. It may or may not be practicable to secure at the close of hostilities and as part of the settlement an immediate money indemnity from Germany and Austria-Hungary that would satisfy those whose territory has been invaded and whose citizens in civil life have been killed or injured and their property destroyed. Whether it be possible or not to secure such an immediate money indemnity, there is perhaps a better way in which to gain the end which France properly seeks. It might readily be provided that claims of this kind should be submitted to an impartial International Court of Justice, whose findings would be final. The evidence that Germany has time and time again violated the laws of war and the provisions of the Hague Conventions, to say nothing of the laws of humanity, is quite overwhelming. It is just because this evidence is so overwhelming that those who have been injured can afford, in the interest of a durable peace, to have their claims judicially determined rather than to force the collection of an indemnity by sheer weight of military power. What the world most thinks of and what the belligerents themselves should most think of is how the settlement of this conflict is to affect the future of mankind. Where there are two ways of achieving the same end, one a conventional way for which there are many precedents, and the other an unconventional way which seeks to set an example of better things, then the same spirit which has animated and directed France in its military effort and in its literally colossal work of national organization may guide it to choose a course which will most certainly help to define and to secure the ideals for which it has been carrying on this amazing struggle.

Whatever may be said of the horrors and atrocities of the present war, surely one of its most remarkable by-products is its effect on the national mind, the national conscience, and the national will of France. The best in France has come to the surface everywhere, and it will probably never be possible for the nation to lose the good effects and the stimulating results of its effort to maintain its integrity and to defend its liberty. During the epoch-making days at Vienna in 1815, Talleyrand was in the habit of describing as "a good European," any statesman who was capable of conceiving the State system of the Western World as a whole. The people of France and French statesmen generally are and long have been good Europeans in Talleyrand's sense. This characteristic of the French people increases the likelihood that they will throw the weight of their great influence and example in favor of the establishment, on sound foundations, of a new European order. It was their own Joubert who so finely said: "Force and Right are the governors of this world; Force till Right is ready."

There remains the restitution of French territory which is or may be occupied by the enemy. So far as concerns those northern and northeastern departments which are at the moment occupied by German military forces, the matter is a comparatively simple one. Germany will assuredly be glad enough to retire from present French territory as a condition of peace. The question of Alsace-Lorraine, however, which became what the Germans call Reichsland after the war of 1870, is not quite so simple.

VII

THERE are some public questions which are so wrapped in sentiment that they cannot be helpfully treated solely from the standpoint of abstract argument. The future of Alsace-Lorraine is distinctly such a question. For forty-four years the symbolic statue of Strasbourg in the Place de la Concorde, surrounded as it has been by pathetic evidences of the mournful feeling of the French people, has borne eloquent testimony to this fact. Should it be said that the future of Alsace-Lorraine is to be settled on the strict principles of nationality, and that if so settled the issue would be in large part favorable to France, the answer is that unless France herself were satisfied there would remain planted in the very heart of Europe the seeds either of another international war or of long generations of international suspicion, hostility, and unhappiness.

In 1870 Mr. Gladstone supported in the British Cabinet the view that the transfer of Alsace and Lorraine from French to German sovereignty without reference to the populations could not be regarded in principle as a question between the two belligerents only, since it involved considerations of

legitimate interest to all the Powers of Europe. He
pointed out its bearing upon the Belgian question
and upon those principles which were likely to be of
great consequence in the eventual settlement of the
Eastern question.

The deputies from Alsace and Lorraine who had
seats in the French National Assembly convoked
at Bordeaux to settle terms of peace with Germany
left no one in doubt as to the wishes of those whom
they represented.   On February 17, 1871, these
deputies presented to the National Assembly this
ringing declaration, which had been submitted to
Gambetta and which had the approval of Victor
Hugo, Louis Blanc, Edgar Quinet, Clemenceau, and
other leading members of the republican party:

Alsace and Lorraine are opposed to alienation. . . .
These two provinces, associated with France for more than
two centuries in good and in evil fortune, and constantly ex-
posed to hostile attack, have consistently sacrificed themselves in the cause of national greatness.   They have sealed
with their blood the indissoluble compact that binds them
to French unity.   Under the present menace of foreign pretensions, they affirm their unshakable fidelity in the face
of all obstacles and dangers, even under the yoke of the in-
vader. With one accord citizens who have remained in their
homes, as well as soldiers who have hastened to join the
colors, proclaim, the former by their votes and the latter
by their action in the field, to Germany and to the world
the unalterable determination of Alsace and of Lorraine to
remain French territory.   France cannot consent to or determine by treaty the cession of Alsace and Lorraine. . . .
We now proclaim as forever inviolable the right of Alsatians
and Lorrainers to remain members of the French nation,

and we pledge ourselves, our compatriots, our children, **and** our children's children, to vindicate that right through all time and by all possible ways in the face of those who usurp authority over us.

Nevertheless the National Assembly, under the constraint of overwhelming military defeat, accepted the treaty of peace on March 1.

It was a solemn and pathetic moment when, before withdrawing from the National Assembly, the deputies from Alsace and from Lorraine read out their famous Protest of Bordeaux:

We, who, in defiance of all justice, have been given over by an odious abuse of power to foreign domination, have a last duty to perform. We declare a compact which disposes of us without our consent null and void. It will ever remain open to each and all of us to claim our rights in such manner and in such measure as conscience shall dictate. . . . Our brothers of Alsace and Lorraine, now cut off from the common family, will preserve their filial affection for the France now absent from their homes until the day when she returns to take her place there again.

At a moment's notice intelligent populations which had been French for centuries, and whose French patriotism and loyalty were most fervent, were compelled to accept a new sovereignty and to assent, in form at least, to a new allegiance.

Germany misunderstood from the first the nature and extent of her self-imposed task. It was the common belief among Germans that the loyalty of Alsace-Lorraine to France was in large part superficial, and that the beneficent effects of German rule would be so great and so obvious that the populations of these provinces would, in a short time, willingly adjust themselves to the new conditions. The elder von Moltke, whose optimism was not quite so unrestrained as that of some others, thought that Germany would have to remain fully armed for fifty years in order to retain Alsace, but that at the end of that period the Alsatians would cease to wish to be Frenchmen and the question would thus be solved. Time has proved that the fears of Bismarck, the statesman, as to the wisdom of this annexation were better justified than the confidence of von Moltke, the strategist.

The fifty years have nearly passed. The policy of semi-military occupation and of stern repression has produced the natural, but not the expected, results. There can be no reasonable doubt that the great body of the population of Alsace and of Lorraine eagerly await the day when these provinces will be restored to their place in the French Republic.

There is little to be gained from following the course of learned historical discussions as to matters five hundred or even a thousand years old in the history of this territory. As a matter of fact, if appeal be made to history, then it must be admitted that away back in the Middle Ages Alsace, although speaking a Germanic dialect, was within the range of the influence and under the domination of French culture. It is probably the case that the Gothic artists who built the cathedral at Strasbourg either came from the Ile de France or had gained their

inspiration there. Politically speaking, this territory had been for hundreds of years an object of
continual strife between the nations which it was
supposed to hold safely apart. It was in the very
dubious and dangerous position of a small buffer
state at a time when the impulse to territorial ex-
pansion and to the extension of dynastic authority
ran strong and high. When at the close of the
Thirty Years' War Alsace sought protection from a
more powerful state than the Holy Roman Empire
had shown itself to be, it came under the protection
of France at the request of its own people. The
French Revolution and its accompanying wars com-
pleted the incorporation of Alsace in France and
solidified in many ways the political relationship already a century and a half old.

There is little use in threshing over old straw now,
but the forcible wresting of Alsace-Lorraine from
France in 1871 was a public injury which must now
be repaired in the only way that it can be repaired,
namely, by the return of these provinces to France
where they belong and where they wish to be. This
is, as Mr. Gladstone said, a matter which affects
the interests not of France and of Germany alone,
but those of all Europe and indeed of the whole world.

The war of 1870 had two immediate results: one,
the unification of Germany, which was a good result;
the second, the separation of Alsace-Lorraine from
France, which was an evil result. He would be a
hardy man who to-day would claim that the holding
of Alsace-Lorraine as Reichsland has contributed to

German unity, and he would be a blind man who could not see that if a durable peace is to follow this war, then Alsace-Lorraine must go back to France. As to this, appeal might be made to Treitschke himself, for in speaking of Napoleon's policy of world conquest he said: "Such a naked policy of conquest in the long run destroys its own instruments. . . . It presumes to take possession of countries which cannot be fitted into the national state as living members."

One need go no farther to find a justification of the demand of France for the return of Alsace-Lorraine. If and when they finally admit defeat on the field of battle, Germany and her allies assent to the return of Alsace-Lorraine to France, they will have given the strongest possible evidence, which the world will heartily welcome, of their desire and intention to assist in making and in preserving a peace that will be durable because it is just. It is futile to suggest as an alternative the incorporation of Alsace-Lorraine in the German Empire with rights of autonomy. It is equally futile to propose to obliterate and to overturn old geographical and political distinctions and landmarks by some new alignment of communities. It is futile, too, to suggest that Alsace-Lorraine be erected into an independent state whose neutrality would be guaranteed by her neighbors. All these are ways of not dealing with the problem. In the interest, and as part, of a durable peace Germany must yield back Alsace-Lorraine to France.

VIII

RUSSIA AND THE SLAVS—THE LIBERAL MOVEMENT
IN RUSSIA—THE BOSPORUS AND THE DAR-
DANELLES

TO the Western World, and to Americans in
particular, Russia seems a far-away land. It
is a land of mystery. Its huge size, its geo-
graphic uniformity, its phenomenal natural resources, its heterogeneous populations, its many
and difficult languages and dialects, its unusual
calendar, and its strong religious feeling all give
it a character of its own. Occupying more than
one-sixth of the globe's land surface, Russia constitutes a twentieth-century bridge between the
older East and the newer West, and it combines
in itself striking characteristics of both Orient and
Occident.

Stirrings in the body or in the limbs of this huge
leviathan are long in being recognized and still
longer in being understood by the outside world.
Russia's participation in this war and her direct relation to one of the most important questions that
the war must settle, make it necessary to gain some
notion of the part which she is likely to play in the
world of the future and of what the results of this
war may bring to her.

The Latin, the Anglo-Saxon, and the Teuton

have made their distinctive contributions to our common civilization, and it is already possible to appraise them with some definiteness. The Slav, however, has yet to make his full contribution to the general store of the world's intellectual and political capital. Significant words were spoken by Count Mouravieff when he said: "I believe that Russia has a civilizing mission such as no other people in the world, not only in Asia, but also in Europe. . . . We Russians bear upon our shoulders the new age; we come to relieve the tired men." This is a fine picture and a stirring prophecy.

The present war has not only put hopelessly out of date the various arguments and considerations that have for a century been brought to bear on what Europe knows as the Eastern question, but it has forced to the front with striking clearness the one dominant fact that, in the interest of a durable peace, Russia must control the straits which lead from the Black Sea to the Ægean. Not to give this control to Russia would mean, first, that her people, restless and in large part economically ice-bound, would not feel that the conditions of peace were permanent; and, second, it would mean the possibility of the extension at any future moment of Germany's political system and Machtpolitik to the Balkan Peninsula, to Asia Minor, and beyond. It is just because these facts are clearly understood by the Allies that military and naval operations have been, and are being, carried on in the southeastern theatre of war. The importance which Germany and her allies attach to them is made evident by the fact that commanders of the high competence of Falkenhayn and Mackensen are conducting in person the operations against Rumania.

It has more than once been hinted that the German Emperor holds the conviction that some day the world will divide itself into two great camps, the one speaking the Slavonic and the other speaking the Anglo-Saxon and Germanic tongues, and that the great yellow races of the East will join the Slavs and so bring the world face to face with a contest between two widely different and historically opposed civilizations. If this was a shrewd forecast ten years ago, it is far less likely now. Russia is increasingly Western in thought and in domestic policy. The rigid censorship, more severe than ever since the outbreak of war, keeps from us an exact or complete knowledge of what is taking place in the political and social order of the Russian Empire. It would be no less cruel than ignorant to suppose that Russia is a nation given over entirely to corrupt officials and to a barbarous police, to irreconcilable socialists and to lawbreaking anarchists. Catherine, who in this respect played for Russia somewhat the same part that Frederick the Great did for Prussia, introduced into Russian life and thought some of the personal, literary, and philosophical influences which aided so effectively in bringing on the French Revolution. These influences have been at work in Russia ever since.

They have been colored and modified by the economic and social conditions prevailing there, and they have taken on some of that sombreness and sentiment which are revealed in Russian literature, Russian art, and Russian music. The progress of internal political development has assuredly been slow, and it has met with many and hard setbacks, but with the traditional forms of local self-government to build upon it has in later years made some substantial advances. There can be little doubt that the events and necessities of the war have aided this movement materially, and it is more than probable that when Russia unites with her allies in establishing the terms of a durable peace she will, at the same time, be able to announce significant changes in her internal organization and policies.

Those who have not known Russia may take encouragement from the recent words of M. B. Bourtzeff, active and influential in every Russian progressive movement. "Even we," he wrote, "the adherents of the parties of the Extreme Left, and hitherto ardent anti-militarists and pacifists, even we believe in the necessity of *this* war. *This* war is a war to protect justice and civilization. It will, we hope, be a decisive factor in our united war against war, and we hope that, after it, it will at last be possible to consider seriously the question of disarmament and of universal peace. . . . To Russia this war will bring regeneration. We are convinced that after this war there will no longer be any room for political reaction, and Russia will be associated with the existing group of cultured and civilized countries."

The Tsar's manifesto of October 30, 1905, furnishes the point of departure for further progress in the development and definition of Russian civil liberty. The first article of that manifesto reads: "The population is to be given the inviolable foundation of civil rights based on the actual inviolability of the person, freedom of belief, of speech, of organization, and of meeting." It will, therefore, in all likelihood be a more unified, a more vigorous, as well as a freer and a more tolerant Russia that will emerge from the present conflict. Prince Gorchakof once said: "La Russie ne boude pas; elle se recueille." A kindly and sympathetic world hopefully awaits the result.

It has been said of the Eastern question that it has as many heads as a hydra. The present war has been the Hercules which has cut off all these heads but three. These three remaining heads are: first, the organization of the peoples of the Balkan Peninsula on the basis of nationality under an international guarantee of their national security; second, the erection of a barrier against the possible extension of German Machtpolitik to Asia Minor and its adjoining lands and seas—the Drang nach Osten—and, third, the possession of the Bosporus, the Dardanelles, and the adjoining shores by Russia as a necessary element of her economic independence and her national security.

The first of these topics need not be further discussed.   It is covered by what has already been said as to the application of the principles of nationality and the protection of the rights of small nations.   The second is one of the necessary results of the present war.   From one, and a very important, point of view the Allies are fighting, not the German people, but to prevent the extension over other lands and other peoples of those political theories, doctrines, and practices which the German people have for the time at least made their own.   If there is to be a durable peace, and one which will justify the sacrifices that the Allies have already made, then every door to a systematic and studied extension of Germany's political influence must of necessity be locked.   In Germany this suggestion will be denounced as one more example of the Einkreisungspolitik from which she has already suffered so much.   It must, however, be borne in mind that in these discussions all possible emphasis has been laid upon the maintenance of the open door in international trade.   German trade, therefore, would be in no wise hampered if these suggestions were followed, but the active propaganda in other countries on behalf of German political ideas and German political control would be stopped.   This policy would remove the greatest present cause of war without introducing a new one to take its place.

The third topic appears to be vital to Russia and, therefore, to the peace of the world.   A glance at the map and a modest knowledge of political and economic history will explain the persistence of Russia in seeking access to the seas at points that are open to navigation throughout the year. From her central plains she has thrown out three arms or tentacles, one of prodigious length, with a view to the uninterrupted use of the ocean highways by her commerce. The Trans-Siberian Railway has been thrown across the steppes of Asia in order to reach the Pacific. Russia's diplomacy in regard to Persia, to British India, and to Turkey has steadily had in mind to secure an outlet to the waters of the Persian Gulf. The third arm or tentacle is reaching out through the Black Sea to the Bosporus and the Dardanelles. With Russia established there, under the international conditions which these discussions propose, her economic independence would be secure, the world's sources of food supply would be greatly increased, and the principles for which the Allies are fighting would gain a material guarantee of the first importance.

It is already assumed in Russia that both England and France will agree, at the conclusion of the war, to the annexation by Russia both of Constantinople and of the adjoining straits. In March, 1915, the important liberal journal of Moscow, *Russkia Viédomosti*, published an article by Prince Eugène Troubetzkoï, which is known to have exercised a very strong influence in Russia, and to have given expression to the prevailing opinion among all classes in the empire. Prince Troubetzkoï flatly says that the only solution which fairly meets

the nation's interests is that Constantinople and the
straits should become Russian. A like opinion has
been expressed by M. Milioukoff, whose leading
position among the Russian Liberals is well known.

It would appear, then, that before long some of
the most serious blunders of both British and Russian diplomacy in the nineteenth century may be
remedied and the whole world be the gainer thereby. Mr. Gladstone assailed Lord Beaconsfield and
Lord Salisbury for having spoken at the Berlin
Congress in 1878 in the tones of Metternich, and
not in the tones of Mr. Canning, of Lord Palmerston,
and of Lord Russell. He insisted that their voice
was not heard in unison with the institutions, the
history, and the character of England. Was he
wrong?

IX

PRUSSIAN MILITARISM—ITS BASIS AND ITS CAUSE—
HOW FAR IT MAY BE CONTROLLED BY CON-
QUEST

THE ground that has now been traversed includes the outline of a settlement of the
issues of the war that would secure the free
national development of every state whether great
or small, the policy of the open door in international
trade, the exemption of private property at sea,
other than contraband, from capture or destruction,
and that would restore Alsace-Lorraine to France
as well as make Russia mistress of the Dardanelles
and the Bosporus. There is one other subject
mentioned by Mr. Asquith in his Guildhall Declaration, but not referred to by Viscount Grey, which is
constantly in the minds of the Allies, and which
never fails to be mentioned when conditions of a
lasting peace are discussed. In Mr. Asquith's own
words: "We shall never sheathe the sword, which we
have not lightly drawn, . . . until the military
domination of Prussia is wholly and finally destroyed." Mr. Asquith chooses his words, and particularly his adjectives and adverbs, with more
scrupulous care than any other statesman of our
time. His statement, therefore, is of primary importance.

Prussian military domination rests first upon

Prussia's military policy and its fixed habit of thinking of all questions of foreign policy in terms of military power and of that alone, as well as upon the vast population of the German Empire which supplies the needed men to keep in effective organization huge armies ready to move at command. The fact that Prussia has a system of universal training and universal military service has little or nothing to do with its military domination. Switzerland has substantially the same thing, and no one thinks of the Swiss as other than a people devoted to the ways of peace. A Swiss army of the same size as that of Prussia would not give to Switzerland the military domination which Prussia has until just now enjoyed. The reason is that military domination does not consist chiefly, or indeed at all, in potential military power, but rather in the attitude of the public mind toward the military system and the army, and in the relative importance assigned to force and to right in weighing and deciding upon matters of international policy. In other words, militarism is a state of mind. Prussian militarism is a Prussian state of mind, and in so far as the German people as a whole have accepted the Prussian state of mind as a sound or as a necessary one Germany is just now a militaristic nation. Of course, this was not always so. The South German people from time immemorial have been poets and artists, kindly and gentle in their manners and without overruling ambitions to conquer and to reform the world. The Prussian hegemony, while certainly necessary to bring about and to insure German unity, has brought not a few evils in its train. One of the chief of these is the extension to the South German folk of the Prussian point of view together with Prussian leadership.

The history of Prussia is a record of extraordinary success in making the most of a meagre beginning, and in extending Prussian rule by sheer force of will, might, and administrative effectiveness. Prussia may well be proud of her accomplishment during the past hundred years, both in creating a new and highly efficient administrative system and in extending her influence and rule over other members of the Germanic family. Prussia has always been a militaristic state, and has never put off the military uniform even when creating and developing a stupendous industrial and commercial system. Prussia has always conceived of history as a struggle between either the Teuton and the Slav, the Teuton and the Frank, the Teuton and the Anglo-Saxon, or the Teuton and somebody else. She always thinks of the Teuton as fighting. She studies her neighbors not in terms of friendship and co-operation, but in terms of rivalry and fear. These have always been the characteristics of Prussia; and as the modern European system developed, and Prussian thought came under the control of a new and almost ecstatic political philosophy which placed Prussia at the pinnacle of history's greatness, sharply marked off by its inherent superiority from the remaining world, it was but a short step to the conviction, perfectly sincere, that it would be good for the remaining world to be brought under the domination of the Prussian political philosophy. To a normal Prussian the army seemed the best and most natural agent for use in this process of world salvation. Men otherwise sober and self-contained, scholars otherwise learned and highly trained, men of affairs otherwise practical and shrewd to the point of cunning, became enamoured of the vista which was thus spread out before them. When Houston Chamberlain told the Prussians that they were the modern elect, his tribute was received as a matter of course and as being fully deserved. To the onlooker there is in all this an absence of saving humor to a degree that is almost incredible; nevertheless it is the combination of Prussian history, Prussian pride, Prussian political philosophy, and Prussian lack of humor that has created what is known as Prussian militarism. It is this curiously composite and elusive but yet terribly real thing which Mr. Asquith demands shall be brought to an end.

How can this be done? Prussian military domination is ended as far as the rest of the world is concerned when the German armies are defeated, and when the military force of the Allies proves itself adequate not only to restrain the German armies from further advance, but to drive them back upon their own territory broken and defeated. This, however, can hardly be the whole of the end which Mr. Asquith has in mind. So far as Prussian militarism is a menace to Europe because of its power, its zeal, and its determination in attack, it can and will be restrained by the outcome of this war. In so far, however, as Prussian militarism is a state of mind it cannot be exorcised by any forcible process whatsoever. It can be got rid of only by a change of heart on the part of the German people themselves. Herein lies the hope of the future and herein is an essential element of a durable peace.

There is an analogy which Americans should not overlook between the condition in which Prussia will, according to all signs, shortly find itself and the condition in which the Southern States of the American Union were left at the close of the Civil War. Though defeated on the field of battle, the leaders of Southern opinion and the men and women of the South generally never changed their minds as to the justice and correctness of the cause for which they fought so bravely. For a whole generation after Appomattox they spoke of "the lost cause," and while they admitted the cause was lost, they continued to insist that it had been just. After fifty years conditions have so changed that all this is largely a matter of history. Men who fought face to face in the opposing armies can, and often do, discuss with the utmost calmness and in the friendliest possible spirit the causes and issues of the conflict that shook the Union to its foundations from 1861–5. The lesson would appear to be that when Germany is defeated she will not of necessity—and, indeed, probably will not at all—change her mind as to the correctness of her position in this war and as to the justice of her cause. But, as in the case of the South, after a half-century has passed this will be only a matter of academic discussion and debate. Prussian militarism will be overthrown so far as the Allies' armies can overthrow it when Germany is brought to join in arrangements for a durable peace on the basis of justice.

The German people themselves must do the rest. It is probably true that whatever may have been the German Emperor's personal preferences in July, 1914, this war would never have taken place had the revolutionary movement of 1848 resulted differently in Germany. The failure of that movement, involving as it did the emigration to America of a considerable body of German Liberals and the slow elimination from German public life of that powerful and constructive type of Liberal found in every other European country, left Germany without the strong impulse toward democratic policies which the revolution of 1688 gave to England and the revolution of 1789 to France. With the disappearance of the German Liberal the line of demarcation between the ultra-Conservative on the one hand and the advanced Socialist on the other became increasingly sharp, and under the benign possibilities of the Prussian electoral system and of the Imperial German Constitution the power of the ultra-Conservative element has been maintained even in the face of a large increase in the number of Socialists. It is this ultra-Conservative element in Germany, with its dominant philosophy of life and of politics, that has come into conflict with the liberal nations of the Western World. Just as Napoleon by the sheer force of his personality and his military genius gathered into his own hands for twenty years all the power and the energy of post-revolutionary France, so the ultra-Conservative Prussian has gathered into his hands for more than twenty years all the power and energy of non-revolutionized Germany.

Following Waterloo, Napoleon's throne quickly tottered and fell. After a few years of stagnation and reaction France resumed its forward post-revolutionary progress until it became the French Republic of to-day. A similar development doubtless lies before Prussia and the German people. They themselves must determine what the form and the spirit of their own government are to be, and no other nation or group of nations, however completely victorious, can undertake to change it for them without throwing away the very principles for which the war is being waged by them. The victory over Prussian militarism considered as a state of mind, and the making over of non-revolutionized Germany into a more liberal and more democratic state, are tasks for the German people themselves. There is no compulsory road to repentance. It is incredible that a people of their intellectual force, discipline, power of organization, and scientific competence should not in due time view the democratic movement precisely as France and Great Britain have viewed it. When this comes about, Germany will displace her Machtpolitik for the Interessenpolitik upon which Bismarck laid such constant stress. She will, to use another of Bismarck's striking phrases, again justly measure "das Gewicht der Imponderabilien," and moral law will be recognized as applying to the conduct of her public policies as well as to that of her private life.

It is true that Prussian militarism must be wholly and finally destroyed before the peace of the world will be really secure, but inasmuch as it can only be wholly and finally destroyed by the German people themselves, the war need not be continued until that end is accomplished. All that the Allies can do toward the destruction of Prussian military domination is to confine it to Germany. When so confined it will disappear not slowly, but relatively fast by reason of its own weight and untimeliness.

There is, however, one way in which Prussian militarism might emerge victorious even if the German armies are finally defeated on the field of battle—that is, if the spirit and policies of Prussian militarism should conquer the mind of Great Britain or that of any other allied Power. A Hymn of Hate is as unlovely when sung in English as when sung in German. The destruction of liberal policies and practices under the guise of national necessity differs but little from "die Not kennt kein Gebot," with which Chancellor von Bethmann-Hollweg defended the ravishing of Belgium. The Allies, and particularly Great Britain, have urgent need to be on their guard that when they are defeating Prussian militarism on the field of battle, it does not gain new and striking victories over them in the field of ideas. A durable peace requires that Prussian militarism be wholly and finally destroyed; first, by the allied armies in the field; second, by the German people in their domestic policies; and, third, by the allied Powers in keeping it from invading their own political systems.

X

THE FUNDAMENTAL PRINCIPLES OF A NEW INTER-
NATIONAL ORDER—THE RIGHTS AND DUTIES OF
NATIONS—THE INTERNATIONAL MIND—INTER-
NATIONAL LAW AS NATIONAL LAW

AFTER what has gone before, it is not necessary to pass in extended review those aspects of a durable peace which are of most
immediate concern to Italy and to what may,
without disrespect, be termed the other minor
belligerent Powers. If it is reasonable to expect
Great Britain, France, and Russia to make their
own the principles and policies already laid down,
and if it is also reasonable to expect Germany to
accept them—save in so far as the giving up of
Alsace-Lorraine to France, the assumption by
Russia of jurisdiction over the Bosporus and the
Dardanelles, and the restriction of what is called
Prussian militarism to the German Empire, there
to be dealt with by the German people in their
own way and in their own time, are compulsory as
the price of peace when the military victory of the
Allies is admitted—then it is time to consider the
foundations of a new international order sanctioned
and protected by international law and supported
by an international guarantee so definite and so
powerful that it cannot and will not be lightly attacked or shaken in the future by any Power.

This new international order will, it is hoped and believed, justify the assertion which Mr. Gladstone made, too confidently as it proved, nearly fifty years ago, when he said: "The greatest triumph of our time has been the enthronement of the idea of public right as the governing idea of European politics."

There can be no question that the idea of public right has taken strong root in the minds of the smaller nations and in those of Great Britain and France as well. Following this war it will be the opportunity and the duty of every lover of liberty, of justice, and of peace to labor to extend the rule of public right not alone over the politics of Europe, but over those of the whole world.

In order to find a point of beginning there must be an agreement, assented to by all the great Powers, including the United States and Japan, as to what are the fundamental rights and duties of nations. On January 6, 1916, the American Institute of International Law, consisting of representatives of every one of the American republics in session at Washington, adopted a statement as to the rights and duties of nations which it would be hard to improve. It is this:

1. Every nation has the right to exist, and to protect and to conserve its existence; but this right neither implies the right nor justifies the act of the state to protect itself or to conserve its existence by the commission of unlawful acts against innocent and unoffending states.

2. Every nation has the right to independence in the sense

that it has a right to the pursuit of happiness and is free to develop itself without interference or control from other states, provided that in so doing it does not interfere with or violate the rights of other states.

3. Every nation is in law and before law the equal of every other nation belonging to the society of nations, and all nations have the right to claim and, according to the Declaration of Independence of the United States, "to assume, among the Powers of the earth, the separate and equal station to which the laws of nature and of nature's God entitle them."

4. Every nation has the right to territory within defined boundaries and to exercise exclusive jurisdiction over its territory, and all persons, whether native or foreign, found therein.

5. Every nation entitled to a right by the law of nations is entitled to have that right respected and protected by all other nations, for right and duty are correlative, and the right of one is the duty of all to observe.

6. International law is at one and the same time both national and international: national in the sense that it is the law of the land and applicable as such to the decision of all questions involving its principles; international in the sense that it is the law of the society of nations and applicable as such to all questions between and among the members of the society of nations involving its principles.

Should this declaration be generally agreed to, and should the necessary steps be taken to make it effective, it will hardly be disputed that as the outcome of the present war the world will be carried further forward on the road to a durable peace than even the most optimistic would have thought possible a decade ago. At the same time care must be taken not to put too much reliance upon formal declarations and upon the machinery of even the most approved international system. More important than the declaration of rights and duties of nations, and more important than the machinery which may be erected to give that declaration vitality and force, is the spirit of the peoples who unite in taking these steps. What the world is waiting for and what it must achieve before the foundations of a durable peace are securely laid is what Nicholas Murray Butler has called the international mind, which he defines as "nothing else than that habit of thinking of foreign relations and business, and that habit of dealing with them, which regard the several nations of the civilized world as friendly and co-operating equals in aiding the progress of civilization, in developing commerce and industry, and in spreading enlightenment and culture throughout the world."

Once this point of view is gained and this code of international morals accepted, then all dreams of world conquest will fade forever, as well as all schemes to extend Anglo-Saxon, or Latin, or Teutonic, or Slavonic culture over the whole world. The several stones in the structure of civilization will differ in size, in character, and in the weight that they support, but each one of them will do its part.

The several nations now at war and those neutral nations that will join them in bringing about a new international order could do no better than adopt as their platform the eloquent words of the declaration made by Elihu Root when Secretary of State of the United States in the presence of the official delegates of the American republics accredited to the third Pan American Conference held at Rio de Janeiro on July 31, 1906, which stirred the heart of every American republic and which sounded the note of a genuinely new international freedom:

> We wish for no victories but those of peace, for no territory except our own, for no sovereignty except the sovereignty over ourselves. We deem the independence and equal rights of the smallest and weakest member of the family of nations entitled to as much respect as those of the greatest empire, and we deem the observance of that respect the chief guarantee of the weak against the oppression of the strong. We neither claim nor desire any rights, or privileges, or powers that we do not freely concede to every American republic. We wish to increase our prosperity, to expand our trade, to grow in wealth, in wisdom, and in spirit, but our conception of the true way to accomplish this is not to pull down others and profit by their ruin, but to help all friends to a common prosperity and a common growth, that we may all become greater and stronger together.

The declaration that international law is at one and the same time both national and international has far-reaching and very practical significance for the work of building a new international order. The courts of Great Britain, beginning with Lord Chancellor Talbot in 1733, and including Lord Chief Justice Mansfield in 1764, have held that the law of nations is part of the common law of England. Sir William Blackstone supported this doctrine in his classic commentaries. This doctrine holds good as well in the United States as in Great Britain, a fact to which both Thomas Jefferson and Alexander Hamilton bore convincing testimony. In the lifetime of the present generation the United States Supreme Court has held that international law is part of our law, and that, in order to ascertain and administer it in cases where there is no treaty and no controlling executive or legislative act or judicial decision, resort must be had to the customs and usages of civilized nations. A sufficient legal basis is, therefore, already at hand for the bringing into being at the close of the war of a new international order that will include the United States in its scope. An international order of the effective kind here contemplated calls for the establishment of an International Court of Justice. The next step, then, is to discuss the constitution and the functions of such a court and to recall what progress had been made before August 1, 1914, toward bringing it into existence.

XI

WORK OF THE FIRST HAGUE CONFERENCE—DIS-
ARMAMENT AND ARBITRATION—THE COURT OF
ARBITRAL JUSTICE

SPEAKING as a member of the second Peace
Conference at The Hague on August 1, 1907,
Mr. Joseph H. Choate closed his address in
support of the American project for a permanent
court of arbitral justice with these words: "We
have done much to regulate war, but very little
to prevent it. Let us unite on this great pacific
measure and satisfy the world that this second
Conference really intends that hereafter peace, and
not war, shall be the normal condition of civilized
nations." Mr. Choate's language may well serve
as the text for a discussion of the form and jurisdiction of such an International Court of Justice as
will contribute most powerfully to a durable peace.

It is desirable to make clear the important distinction between a real court and an arbitral tribunal, and not to permit ourselves to confuse the one
with the other.

The history of the principle of international
arbitration and its various applications is a long
and interesting one, but it is not necessary to re-
count or to examine it here. At the first Peace
Conference at The Hague international arbitration
was not originally a matter of main concern. The

Russian circular note proposing that Conference, which was held in 1899, dealt almost entirely with the desirability of reducing armaments or at least of checking their rapid growth. In a few striking sentences this note, which, coming from Russia, took the whole world by surprise, pointed out how national culture, economic progress, and the production of wealth were being either paralyzed or perverted in their development by the huge expenditures upon "terrible engines of destruction, which though to-day regarded as the last word in science are destined to-morrow to lose all value in consequence of some fresh discovery in the same field." Moreover, continued the note, "in proportion as the armaments of each Power increase so do they less and less attain the object aimed at by the Governments. . . . It appears evident, then, that if this state of affairs be prolonged it will inevitably lead to the very cataclysm which it is desired to avert, and the impending horrors of which are fearful to every human thought." In this note the subject of arbitration was not specifically mentioned, although it may fairly be urged that the principle of the judicial settlement of international disputes was latent in the expression of the hope that such a Conference as was proposed would result in an agreement among the nations to unite in "a solemn avowal of the principles of equity and law, upon which repose the security of states and the welfare of peoples." If the nations are to agree upon an avowal of belief in certain controlling principles of equity and law, then it would seem that they must be prepared to construct an institution for the application of these principles to specific cases of international difference, and such an institution could only be what the world knows as a court.

When the adhesion of the leading Powers had been secured to the principle that such an international Conference as the Russian Government proposed should be held, Count Mouravieff, Russian Foreign Minister, submitted a programme for the Conference containing eight topics. The last of these related to the acceptance in principle of the use of good offices, mediation, and voluntary arbitration in cases where they were available with the purpose of preventing armed conflict between nations, together with an understanding in relation to their mode of application, and the establishment of a uniform practice in applying them. As the event proved, it was this topic and not any question of the reduction of armaments that most engaged the attention of the first Hague Conference. It was quickly felt, not only by the delegates to the Conference, but by the public opinion of the whole world, that, generous and humane as were the motives of the Tsar in inviting an international Conference to consider a limitation of armaments, this question did not furnish either the wisest or the most practical mode of approach to the solution of the problem of establishing a new international order by means of which peace would be better secured. It was seen and generally admitted that armaments are themselves an effect and not a cause, that they are the instruments with which war is waged, but that armaments alone do not declare or directly provoke war. Therefore to attempt to limit armaments, while leaving untouched the real causes of war and the real incentives to international jealousy and hostility, would be to put the cart before the horse.

By such a policy war would not be prevented, but it would be carried on, in all probability, at a greatly increased cost in human life and human treasure because of the necessity of improvising at short notice a great series of military and naval instrumentalities with which to conduct a war that was the outgrowth of international jealousy, international ambition, or international greed. There can be no doubt that a competitive race in armaments among nations is an economic and moral disorder that has the gravest consequences, but the way in which to cure that disorder is to strike at its causes and not merely at its symptoms. Its causes lie deep in human nature and in national pride and ambition. There is no practical way to lessen the likelihood of international war and to insure a consequent steady diminution in military and naval armaments except one which will bring the public opinion of the great nations of the world more and more to the support of the principle that international differences may and should be judicially examined and determined.

For these reasons the work of the first Hague Conference is not only commendable, but stands as a notable landmark in the history of the progress of better international relations. Americans, Englishmen, and Frenchmen may well be proud that in establishing that Court of Arbitral Justice, which was the chief permanent result of the first Hague Conference, the initiative was taken and the greatest influence in carrying the project to a successful issue exercised by Doctor Andrew D. White and Frederick W. Holls, Chairman and Secretary, respectively, of the American delegation; by Lord, then Sir Julian, Pauncefote, Chairman of the British delegation; and by MM. Léon Bourgeois, d'Estournelles de Constant, and Renault, the three chief representatives of the French Republic. Doctor White's personal letter to von Bülow, then Imperial German Chancellor, written under date of June 16, 1899, may well prove to be one of the most important documents in modern diplomatic history. That letter, together with the personal influence in Germany of Doctor White and of Mr. Holls, who was its bearer, persuaded the German Emperor and the Chancellor to withdraw their opposition to any recognition of the principle of arbitration and so secured the adhesion of Germany to the final act of the Conference. When a real International Court of Justice comes to be established, it may be found that the support both of official Germany and of German public opinion, if given, may be traceable in large part to the action taken by the German Emperor and his Chancellor in 1899, at the urgent and most persuasive solicitation of Doctor White.

The first Hague Conference did not really establish a court in the sense in which that word is generally understood, but it did make great progress toward the establishment of such a court, and toward preparing the public mind for farther and more definite steps. It was no small achievement to have the powers unite, as they then did, in the declaration that they would use their best efforts to insure the pacific settlement of international differences with a view to obviating as far as possible recourse to force in the relations between states. They agreed upon admirable provisions for good offices and mediation as well as for international commissions of inquiry. They defined international arbitration as having for its object "the settlement of disputes between states by judges of their own choice and on the basis of respect for law." It will at once be seen how far this falls short of the settlement of disputes between states by judges independently chosen, and on the basis not alone of respect for law, but of submission to law. The permanent Court of Arbitration was really nothing more than a panel of men "of known competency in questions of international law, of the highest moral reputation and disposed to accept the duties of arbitrators." Such a tribunal as this, wholly dependent for its existence and usefulness upon the concurrence of two disagreeing states in submitting a question to arbitration and in agreeing to the choice of individual arbitrators, was not a true court. Nevertheless its importance must not be minimized, for this tribunal has dealt with not a few cases of more than usual difficulty, and it has served to accustom the public opinion of the civilized world to the spectacle of sovereign nations submitting international disputes which had not been resolved by the usual diplomatic means to inquiry and judgment by arbitrators.

Mexico and the United States, at the instance of President Roosevelt, quickly submitted to this tribunal the Pious Fund Case. Shortly afterward Germany, Great Britain, and Italy brought before it in the Venezuelan Preferential Case their controversy with the Republic of Venezuela over certain pecuniary claims of their subjects. Similarly France, Germany, and Great Britain submitted to the Hague Tribunal their difference with Japan over a matter arising from the extraterritorial jurisdiction which prior to 1894 was maintained in respect to the citizens of foreign nations resident in Japan. The Casablanca Case between France and Germany and the Savarkar Case between France and Great Britain were similarly considered and decided. Doubtless the most important case yet heard by this tribunal was the North Atlantic Coast Fisheries Case, in which Great Britain and the United States were opposing parties in a vexatious controversy that had lasted for one hundred years.

It will be seen, therefore, that while the nations have not yet established a real International Court of Justice, they have taken such long steps toward it that it should not be difficult to cover the remaining distance, in view of the vital importance of the existence of such a court to an international order which aims to secure a durable peace.

XII

A VIGOROUS attempt to add a real International Court of Justice to the permanent
Court of Arbitration that was established
at The Hague by the Conference of 1899 was made
at the second Hague Conference, which met in 1907.
This was largely due to the urgent insistence of the
American delegation. Their action was taken under
the explicit instructions of Secretary Root, and it
achieved a far larger measure of success than is
generally understood. The point then reached in
the establishment of a court is the point at which
to begin when this war is ended.

In his formal instructions to the American delegates to that conference Mr. Root pointed out that
the principal objection to arbitration rests not upon
the unwillingness of nations to submit their controversies to impartial arbitration, but upon an
apprehension that the arbitrations to which they
submit them may not be really impartial. In other
words, he pressed upon the American delegates, and

through them upon the conference, a clear recognition of the distinction between the action of judges deciding questions of fact and law upon the record before them under a sense of judicial responsibility, and the action of negotiators effecting settlement of questions brought before them in accordance with the traditions and usages and subject to all the considerations and influences which affect diplomatic agents. The one is a judicial determination of a disputed question; the other is an attempt to satisfy both contending parties by arriving at some form of compromise. Secretary Root pointed to the Supreme Court of the United States, passing with impartial and impersonal judgment upon questions arising between citizens of the different States or between foreign citizens and citizens of the United States, as a type of tribunal to which the nations of the world would be much more ready than now to submit their various controversies for decision. He instructed the American delegates to make an effort to bring about a development of the existing Hague Tribunal into a permanent court composed of judges who are judicial officers and nothing else, who are paid adequate salaries, who have no other occupation, and who will devote their entire time to the trial and decision of international causes by judicial methods and under a sense of judicial responsibility. He pointed out that the members of such a court should be selected from different countries in such manner that the different systems of law and procedure and the principal languages would be fairly represented. It was Secretary Root's expressed hope that this court might be made of such dignity, consideration, and rank that the best and ablest jurists would accept appointment to it, and that the whole world would have absolute confidence in its judgments.

There have been no better definition and description than those given by Secretary Root of that International Court of Justice which is an essential part of any international order that will have a durable peace as its aim. Before such a court can be brought into existence, however, it is necessary to remove the fears and doubts of those who question whether such a court could really be impartial, and therefore judicial. The American, with the example of the United States Supreme Court before him, and with that conception of an independent judiciary which removes judges from executive or political control and which gives them authority not only to settle disputes between individuals but to protect the individual and his constitutional rights against invasion by the executive and the legislature themselves, has little difficulty in grasping the conception of an independent and impartial international court. This has also become easier for the subject of Great Britain as the later developments in the history of the Judicial Committee of the Privy Council have shown him grave questions of constitutional and international law that arise in all parts of the empire being judicially settled by that body sitting at Westminster.

To understand what is meant by such a court is much more difficult on the part of the citizens or subjects of countries in which the judiciary is really a part of the general administrative system and not an independent body having the authority to pass in review the legality of governmental acts. In countries where courts have no other function than to determine controversies between individuals, and where nations have not progressed to the advanced position of protecting civil and political liberty by judicial process, it is not easy to secure adhesion to a project which contemplates bringing the act of a Government to the bar of judicial inquiry. Probably there is no better or quicker way to bring home to the people of Austria-Hungary, of Germany, and of Russia the purpose and functions of such a court as here described than to establish it in order that its acts and processes may be their own explanation.

It was by the joint efforts of the delegates from Great Britain, Germany, France, and the United States that the project for an International Court of Justice was approved by the second Hague Conference on October 16, 1907. Unfortunately the Conference could not agree upon the method by which the judges of the proposed court were to be chosen. Failure to agree on this vital point deprived the project for the moment of any practical effect. The Conference went so far, however, after having adopted the project, as definitely to recommend that the court be established as soon as the nations could agree upon a method of appointing judges. The German Government has officially declared its readiness to co-operate in the establishment of this court, and the British, French, and American Governments have publicly supported the action of their representatives at The Hague. These significant facts must not be overlooked.

It is important to bear in mind that the action of the second Hague Conference in 1907 was not merely the expression of a wish or desire that a court should be established, but it was a definite recommendation to the Powers to undertake the establishment of the court. Ever since the adjournment of the second Hague Conference it has, therefore, been easy for any group of nations to agree to establish such a court for themselves by coming to a common determination as to how its judges should be appointed. One hope was that an International Prize Court might be called into existence and its jurisdiction gradually enlarged to cover the field of an International Court of Justice. It would now give great satisfaction to the lovers of justice throughout the world if, without waiting for the conclusion of the war, the Governments of the Allied Powers would publicly announce that as one of the terms and conditions of a durable peace they proposed to unite in the prompt establishment of an International Court of Justice substantially as outlined and agreed upon at the second Hague Conference. Such a declaration on their part would emphasize anew the principles of liberty, of order, and of justice for which they are now contending on the field of battle, and would turn the thoughts of men, when terms of peace are discussed, more and more to that justice which must underlie and accompany any peace that is to be durable, and away from that vengeance and reprisal which can only incite to new wars.

To take this step should not be difficult, since the American Government has been pressing it upon all the chief Powers for some years past and has indicated with definiteness and precision how the necessary steps may be taken. The work of the Naval Conference at London in 1908–9 made a beginning in the formulation of some parts of that law which the proposed court must interpret and administer. The war came, however, before an agreement as to the Declaration of London had been finally worked out and all further progress was necessarily suspended. There has never been a clearer demonstration of the truth of the ancient maxim, "Inter arma silent leges."

As late as January 12, 1914, Mr. James Brown Scott, who as Solicitor for the Department of State had been a technical delegate at the second Hague Conference, addressed to Mr. Loudon, Minister of Foreign Affairs of the Netherlands, a letter begging him to take the initiative in bringing about the establishment of a Court of Arbitral Justice through the co-operation of Holland, Germany, the United States, Austria-Hungary, France, Great Britain, Italy, Japan, and Russia. In this letter. which was written with the approval of Mr. Elihu Root and Mr. Robert Bacon, former Secretaries of State, it was pointed out that a court constituted through the co-operation of these nations would, to all intents and purposes, have the advantages and render the services of a true international court, and in a very short time would probably become a court to which every nation would be glad to resort. Before any action could be taken the overhanging war-clouds burst into storm.

It is probable that the plan brought forward by Mr. Scott is the most practicable and, therefore, the one most likely eventually to be followed. An International Court of Justice established by agreement of the nine nations named would have all needed prestige and authority. Should a nation not party to the agreement wish to appear before the court as litigant or be ready to accept an invitation or summons so to appear, it would be easy to provide that in such case the nation in question might appoint an assessor for the hearing of that particular cause. Should a case come before the court involving two or more nations not parties to the agreement for its establishment, then similarly each of those nations might be given the right to name an assessor to participate in hearing the arguments in that case. It is neither necessary nor desirable to go here into further detail as to the constitution and scope of this court. These matters are dealt with in the fullest possible way, and from every point of view in the published records of the

second Hague Conference and in subsequent pub-
lications that deal with this specific question.

Americans must be pardoned if they keep insist-
ing upon the advantage of studying the history and
practice of the Supreme Court of the United States in
order to answer objections and to smooth away difficulties which arise in the minds of many thoughtful
men in other countries as to the practicability of an
International Court of Justice. It may be doubted
whether any strictly legal question as to the rights of
nations and their nationals will arise before such a
court which has not already arisen in some form or
other before the Supreme Court of the United States
as a question involving the rights of States and their
citizens. For example, nearly eighty years ago the
United States Supreme Court was called upon to
distinguish a judicial from a political question; it
did so then and has frequently done so since without serious difficulty. A question addressed to the
framework and political character of a Government
is essentially political; it is, therefore, not a question
that is in its nature justiciable and that can be presented to a court. It would, of course, be necessary
for an International Court of Justice to build up
gradually and by a series of decisions a body of
precedents that would, so to speak, take the form of
an international common law. The point of departure would be the international law of the moment, existing treaties, and the form of agreement
through which the court itself would come into being. It might be expected that this court would de-

cide for itself in matters of doubt whether or not a given question was justiciable. The International Court of Justice could hardly vary from the practice of the United States Supreme Court in not attempting to compel the presence of any Government made defendant or in not attempting to execute by force its finding against the contention of any Government. If the publicity attending the operations of such a court, the inherent and persuasive reasonableness of its findings, and a body of international public opinion that has turned with conviction to the judicial settlement of international disputes, cannot insure the carrying into effect of the judgments of an International Court of Justice, then the world is not ready for such a court. To establish it under such circumstances would merely be to provide another opportunity for so magnifying and sharpening points of international difference as probably to increase the likelihood of war. There was a time when, under great stress of party and personal feeling, Andrew Jackson could say: "John Marshall has made his decision; now let him enforce it." Nevertheless, the judgments of the United States Supreme Court are not only obeyed but respected. This results not alone from the confidence in their reasonableness which the tradition of a century has built up, but from the fact that American public opinion will not tolerate any other course. There is every reason to believe that a course of judicial action that has been demonstrated to be practicable, wise, and beneficent within the

United States will also in time be demonstrated to be practicable, wise, and beneficent as between nations. The important thing is to make a beginning. This the Allies are in position to do.

XIII

SUGGESTED MODE OF PROCEDURE AFTER THE WAR— WORK FOR A THIRD HAGUE CONFERENCE—FOUR SPECIFIC PROPOSALS FOR ACTION

THE natural mode of action on the part of the several Powers at the conclusion of the war would be to arrive, in international conference, at an agreement upon a restatement of the convention for the pacific settlement of international disputes as formulated at the second Hague Conference, and upon the establishment of an International Court of Justice in some such fashion as has been already outlined. In both cases it would be possible to simplify and to improve the forms of statement as these were previously agreed upon. This war has itself made not only possible, but easy, considerable advance beyond the positions then taken. Public opinion understands more clearly than it did at that time what these arrangements involve and how desirable they are. For example, if the International Commissions of Inquiry are to be really valuable, the limitation imposed upon them as to disputes of an international nature that involve either honor or essential interests must be removed. It is a poor sort of international dispute in which some one cannot find a point involving either honor or an essential interest.

At the same time, it is of the first importance to

make no promises that cannot, and will not, be kept by the contracting nations. Therefore, only in so far as the constitution and jurisdiction of the International Court of Justice and the constitution and authority of the International Commissions of Inquiry are understood and assented to by the people of the several nations which enter into them should anything be attempted. To endeavor to do more than this is to hold out a hope that will surely be dashed later to the ground. To attempt a formal international order in advance of anything for which the world is ready might well result in setting back that international order for a generation, or even for a century. The war has prepared the world for much that it would not have accepted three years ago. It is the task of statesmanship to ascertain what instructed public opinion is now willing to support and to fix it in international institutions.

Any international conference to fix the conditions of a durable peace will, as a matter of course, include the United States. The United States is a participant in this war, although an unwilling and a neutral participant. Modern conditions have brought it to pass that a nation may remain neutral and yet be involved, both directly and indirectly, economically and in point of principle, in a war that breaks out on another continent. Moreover, this is no ordinary war. It is, as has been said over and over again, a clash of ideals, of philosophies of life, or political and social aims. This is why it must be fought until the principles at stake are or can be established, and why it cannot be compromised. One who cannot range himself on one side or the other in this conflict must be either so dull of understanding as not to be able to comprehend the greatest things in the world or so profoundly immoral as not to care what becomes of the human race, its liberty, and its progress. To guard against a repetition of any such conflict, representatives of neutral states will undoubtedly be summoned to the same council table with the representatives of the belligerent Powers.

Admirable and far-sighted plans for securing a peaceful international order have been before the world for three hundred years. M. Emeric Crucé submitted his plan, which included liberty of commerce throughout all the world, as early as 1623. Following the Peace of Utrecht, the Abbé de St. Pierre developed his plan, which included mediation, arbitration, and an interesting addition to the effect that any sovereign who took up arms before the union of nations had declared war, or who refused to execute a regulation of the union or a judgment of the Senate, was to be declared an enemy of European society. The union was then to make war upon him until he should be disarmed or until the regulation or judgment should be executed. Some twenty years earlier William Penn had produced his quaint and really extraordinary plan for the peace of Europe, in which he, too, proposed to proceed by military power against any sovereign who refused to submit his claims to a proposed diet, or parliament of Europe, or who refused to abide by and to perform any judgment of such a body. All these plans, like those of Rousseau, Bentham, and Kant, which came later, as well as William Ladd's elaborate and carefully considered essay on a Congress of Nations, published in 1840, were brought into the world too soon. They were the fine and noble dreams of seers which it is taking civilized men three centuries and more to begin effectively to realize.

Out of the international conference that will follow the war there should come, and doubtless will come, a union of states to secure peace. That Mr. Asquith has long had this idea in mind is plain. Speaking at Dublin, on September 25, 1914, when the war was still very young and when German hopes were high and confident, Mr. Asquith, in discussing the causes and meaning of the war, said: "It means, finally, or it ought to mean, perhaps by a slow and gradual process, the substitution for force, for the clash of competing ambitions, for groupings and alliances and a precarious equipoise,—the substitution for all these things of a real European partnership, based on the recognition of equal right and established and enforced by a common will. A year ago that would have sounded like a Utopian idea. It is probably one that may not, or will not, be realized either to-day or to-morrow. If and when this war is decided in favor of the Allies, it will at once come within the range, and before long

within the grasp, of European statesmanship."
Events are hastening the consummation of Mr. Asquith's hope. On November 9 last, Chancellor von
Bethmann-Hollweg said before the main committee
of the Reichstag: "Germany is at all times ready to
join a league of nations—yes, even to place herself
at the head of such a league—to keep in check the
disturbers of the peace." Previously, on May 27,
1916, speaking in Washington, President Wilson had
used these words: "Only when the great nations of
the world have reached some sort of agreement as
to what they hold to be fundamental to their common interest, and as to some feasible method of
acting in concert when any nation or group of nations seeks to disturb those fundamental things,
can we feel that civilization is at least in a way of
justifying its existence and claiming to be finally
established." Similar, if less direct, expressions
have come from responsible statesmen and from
leaders of opinion in other lands. It would seem as
if the world, at the close of this war, would have
within its grasp the possibility to achieve at once a
union of nations to establish an International Court
of Justice to try justiciable causes, International
Commissions of Inquiry to facilitate a solution of
non-justiciable disputes by means of an impartial
and conscientious investigation of the facts and by
making them public, and generally to secure the
peace of the world.

It would be best if the Allied Powers, after the
terms of settlement of the present conflict have

been agreed upon, were themselves to invite such a
conference to meet at The Hague and there to continue to build upon the foundations already laid in
1899 and in 1907. It is natural to expect the Allies
to take the initiative in calling this conference, for
such a step would be in entire accord with the em-
phatic and oft-repeated declarations of their Governments. The powerful participation of France
would assist to realize, so far as is now possible, the
prophetic declaration of Michelet: "Au XXe siècle,
la France déclarera la Paix au monde."

Should the Allies for any reason be reluctant to
invite such a conference, it has been made easy for
the President of the United States to do so. The
Sixty-fourth Congress in enacting the Naval Appro-
priation bill for the current year included the
following provision, which is now the law of the
land:

It is hereby declared to be the policy of the United States
to adjust and settle its international disputes through mediation or arbitration, to the end that war may be honorably
avoided. It looks with apprehension and disfavor upon a
general increase of armament throughout the world, but it
realizes that no single nation can disarm, and that without
a common agreement upon the subject every considerable
power must maintain a relative standing in military strength.

In view of the premises, the President is authorized and
requested to invite, at an appropriate time, not later than
the close of the war in Europe, all the great Governments
of the world to send representatives to a conference which
shall be charged with the duty of formulating a plan for a
court of arbitration or other tribunal, to which disputed

questions between nations shall be referred for adjudication
and peaceful settlement, and to consider the question of
disarmament and submit their recommendation to their
respective Governments for approval.   The President is
hereby authorized to appoint nine citizens of the United
States who, in his judgment, shall be qualified for the mission by eminence in the law and by devotion to the cause of
peace, to be representatives of the United States in such a
conference.   The President shall fix the compensation of
said representatives and such secretaries and other employees
as may be needed.   Two hundred thousand dollars, or so
much thereof as may be necessary, is hereby appropriated
and set aside and placed at the disposal of the President to
carry into effect the provisions of this paragraph.

It may be assumed, therefore, that whether called
by the Governments of the Allied Powers or by the
President of the United States, such a third Hague
Conference will be held as promptly as may be after
the conclusion of hostilities.   Such a conference
will, in effect, be the first step in making a union of
states to secure the peace of the world.   There
should be urged upon it by the delegates from the
United States not only (1) the establishment of the
International Court of Justice, and (2) the International Commissions of Inquiry, already referred to
and described, but (3) the high wisdom of making
provision for the stated and automatic reassembling
of the conference at, say, four-year intervals, and
(4) the adoption, in substance, and so far as possible
in form, of the declaration as to the fundamental
rights and duties of nations that has already been set
out in full in these discussions.   The result of the

action last named would be to give the International Court of Justice a definite and specific statement of fundamental principles to be applied and interpreted in the various causes that will come before it for adjudication.

In all this the United States is at liberty, without departing from its traditional policies or without sacrificing any of its own interests, to participate to the full. In making international law and in establishing an international order for the whole world, the United States is keenly and directly interested. A point of gravest difficulty presents itself, however, when we come to consider the effective enforcement of international law and the effective upholding of whatever international order is established and the relation of the United States thereto. On signing the convention for the pacific settlement of international disputes agreed to at the Hague Conference of 1899 the delegation of the United States made the following formal declaration:

Nothing contained in this convention shall be so construed as to require the United States of America to depart from its traditional policy of not intruding upon, interfering with, or entangling itself in the political questions or policy or internal administration of any foreign state; nor shall anything contained in the said convention be construed to imply a relinquishment by the United States of America of its traditional attitude toward purely American questions.

This reservation was explicitly renewed by the American delegates to the Hague Conference of

1907. Put in plain language, this declaration means that while there is one international law and while there may be one international order, in the declaration and establishment of which the United States participates, yet there are two separate and distinct areas of jurisdiction for the enforcement of international law and for the administration of the international order. The area of one of these jurisdictions is Europe and those parts of Asia and Africa immediately dependent thereon; the area of the second of these jurisdictions is America.

XIV

ENFORCEMENT OF INTERNATIONAL LAW AND THE AD-
MINISTRATION OF A NEW INTERNATIONAL ORDER
—CRITICISM OF THE PROPOSED USE OF FORCE TO
COMPEL SUBMISSION OF EVERY INTERNATIONAL
QUESTION TO A JUDICIAL TRIBUNAL OR COUNCIL
OF CONCILIATION BEFORE BEGINNING HOSTIL-
ITIES—DIFFICULTY OF THE UNITED STATES MAK-
ING ANY AGREEMENT TO THIS END—THE REAL
INTERNATIONAL GUARANTEE FOR NATIONAL SE-
CURITY

B EARING in mind the reservation made by
the delegates of the United States at the
two Hague Conferences, what are likely to
be the methods adopted for the enforcement of international law and for the administration of an
international order, in the establishment of which
the United States participates, and what is likely to
be the relation of the United States thereto? What
are the possible and desirable sanctions of international law and for the findings of an International
Court of Justice?

It will be convenient to discuss the latter question
first.

It may be assumed, perhaps, that what Mazzini
somewhere described as the philosophy of Cain will
no longer find a hearing in the world. In a broad
sense, at least, the nations of the world are their
brothers' keepers. Those principles and policies and

those conditions of human happiness and human progress which are not limited by national boundaries and are not confined by any barriers of race, or religion, or language are not matters of indifference to any people. They are the common interest and the joint concern of all. The analogy between individuals and Governments, and that between states as members of a federal system and nations as co-operating equals in an international order, is illuminating and helpful, but it must not be pressed too far. An individual is a single responsible human being whose deeds may be visited upon his own head. A nation is a large community of individuals holding different personal opinions and having different personal interests, all of whom may or may not agree with and support a given action of their Government, and who cannot therefore be held personally responsible for governmental policy without injustice and unnecessary injury. It is small recompense for the misdeeds of a Government to kill innocent men, women, and children who are its subjects or to ravage and destroy their property. There are serious objections to the use of force as between nations, which objections have nothing to do with pacifist teachings or with the doctrine of non-resistance, but which arise out of the nature of the facts. There is at present no suggestion from any authoritative source that some sort of international sheriff should be called into existence for the purpose of enforcing the findings of an International Court of Justice. It is everywhere proposed to leave this to international public opinion. There are, however, well-supported proposals that, in case any nation which has become a member of the proposed international order shall issue an ultimatum or threaten war before submitting any question which arises to an international judicial tribunal or council of conciliation, it shall be proceeded against forthwith by the other Powers; first, through the use of their economic force, and, second, by the joint use of their military forces if the nation in question actually proceeds to make war or invades another's territory.

In so far as a plan of this kind is a recognition of the undoubted fact that force of some kind is the ultimate sanction in all human affairs, it is on safe ground. When, however, it proposes to make immediate practical application of this principle in the manner described, the case is by no means so clear. It is not unlikely, for example, that the adoption of such a policy would require that every war of whatever character should become in effect a world war. If it be replied that the joint forces of the other Powers would be so overwhelming that no one Power would venture to defy them, then one who recalls the political and military history of Europe must be permitted to doubt. Other matters apart, it is not always so easy to determine to the general satisfaction which of several parties to an agreement is the first aggressor as to warrant the terrible consequences that would follow from treating as an act of aggression on the part of a given nation what that nation considered an act of self-defense, thereby precipitating a world war through the application of the principle in question. If one will take the pains to examine with care the official communications which passed between the various European Governments between July 23 and August 4, 1914, it will be apparent what pains each Government was taking to put some other Government in the wrong. With time to make leisurely examination of the records, the public opinion of the world has made up its mind on these points so far as the present war is concerned. But would it have been practicable, or indeed possible, for a concert of nations to have moved with their joint military forces against Austria-Hungary, or Russia, or Germany in the first days of August, 1914, and have been quite sure of their ground? If it be said that in the presence of such an agreement among the nations as is suggested no such acts of aggression as were committed in the last days of July and the first days of August, 1914, would have taken place, the obvious reply is that this is a very large and a very dangerous assumption.

An even more interesting illustration may be given. On April 20, 1914, the President of the United States in a formal address to the Congress narrated certain circumstances which occurred at Tampico, Mexico, on April 9 and the days next following. Having set forth the facts concerning these incidents, the President continued: "I, therefore, come to ask your approval that I should use

the armed forces of the United States in such ways
and to such an extent as may be necessary to obtain
from General Huerta and his adherents the fullest
recognition of the rights and dignity of the United
States." Two days later the Congress adopted a
joint resolution declaring that the President was
justified in the employment of armed forces of the
United States to enforce his demand for unequivocal
amends for certain affronts and indignities committed against the United States, and at the same
time disclaimed on behalf of the United States any
hostility to the Mexican people or any purpose to
make war upon Mexico. It so happened that between the day of the President's address to the Congress and that of the passage of the joint resolution,
namely, on April 21, the admiral commanding the
American Navy off Vera Cruz, acting under orders,
landed a force of marines at that place and seized
the custom-house. In these operations nineteen
American marines were reported killed and seventy
wounded, while the Mexican loss was reported to be
one hundred and twenty-six killed and one hundred and ninety-five wounded. That legally this
was an act of war can hardly be doubted.

At the time of these incidents there was in existence a treaty between the United States and Mexico
which explicitly provided that any disagreement
arising between the Governments of the two republics should, if possible, be settled in such manner as
to preserve the state of peace and friendship that
existed when the treaty was made, and that if the

two Governments themselves should not be able to come to an agreement a resort should not on that account be had to reprisals, aggression, or hostility of any kind until that Government which deemed itself aggrieved should have maturely considered, in the spirit of peace and good neighborship, whether it would not be better that such difference should be settled by the arbitration of commissioners appointed on each side or by that of a friendly nation. This provision, contained in the Treaty of Guadalupe Hidalgo, proclaimed July 4, 1848, was explicitly reaffirmed in the Gadsden Treaty, proclaimed June 30, 1854.

These being the facts, would it be the contention of those who urge the use of force to compel a power to submit its international disputes to a judicial tribunal or to a council of conciliation before making or threatening war, that had such an agreement been in existence in April, 1914, the armies and navies of Great Britain, of France, of Germany, of Russia, of Italy, and of Japan should have jointly moved against the United States? Would such action, if taken, have been likely to promote international peace or to compel prolonged and destructive international war?

Again, if it be said that with such an agreement in force the Government of the United States would not have taken the action in question, the answer must be that such an inference is, to say the least, exceedingly doubtful.

Those who deal with the facts of international relationships and who refuse to be misled by formulas and mere generalizations must find many reasons to withhold their assent from any plan which under the circumstances just stated would have compelled the various Powers of Europe, with all of whom the United States was on friendly relations, to make joint war upon the American people. It is difficult to contemplate such an event or its possibility having any place in a plan whose aim is to secure a durable peace.

As a matter of fact, the only practical sanction of international law is the public opinion of the civilized world. Even now nations are not anxious to incur the condemnation of other peoples. Such condemnation leads to unfriendliness, and unfriendliness leads to economic and intellectual isolation. These are universally disliked and dreaded. The strongest Governments are the quickest to respond, as a rule, to the judgment of international public opinion. It is in highest degree deplorable that the German Government felt itself strong enough to defy the public opinion of the world in its relation to the origin of the present war and in its conduct of it; but in so doing it departed from the precepts and the practice of Bismarck. He was always anxious that before beginning a war steps should be taken to predispose the opinion of other nations in favor of his policies and acts. That decent respect to the opinions of mankind upon which was rested the first national public act in the Western World is still a powerful moving force among men and nations. It may well be doubted whether this very sanction is not more effective in securing obedience even to municipal law than are the punishments which the various statutes provide. Many a man who would not fear the legal penalty of a wrong act is withheld from it by fear of the terrible punishment which is involved in the loss of the respect and confidence of his fellow men.

So far as the people of the United States are concerned, there would appear to be an almost insuperable obstacle to their joining in an agreement to make war upon a recalcitrant nation which might insist upon beginning hostilities before submitting a dispute to arbitration. There is no higher or more solemn act of sovereignty than the declaration of war. The Constitution of the United States lodges this power in the Congress. Should the United States enter into an international agreement to contribute its military and naval forces to a joint war against some other nation not named, at a time not stated, and under circumstances only generally described, then—waiving all questions of constitutionality—it would have put the power to exercise this solemn sovereign act in commission. After an interval of years, or perhaps of decades, the people of the United States might awake some morning to find themselves at war with Russia, or with Greece, or with Spain, or with Argentina, because of some happening of which they themselves knew little or nothing and on account of which they might well regard going to war as incredible. The chances that under such circumstances an agreement of this kind would be kept are not very great. It ought not, therefore, to be entered into.

In this connection it is worth while recalling the fact that when, on March 18, 1913, President Wilson announced the unwillingness of the United States to participate in the so-called six-power loan to China, he gave as a reason the fact that the responsibility which participation in the loan would involve might go to the length, in some unhappy contingency, of bringing about forcible intervention on the part of the United States in the financial and even in the political affairs of China.

The international guarantee for national security for which the nations, those of Europe in particular, are seeking would be had through the establishment of the institutions and by the declaration of principles that have been already set forth and described. The support and the sanction of these institutions and their guarantees would be the public opinion of the world. By this is meant not the opinion of Governments only, but the instructed and enlightened opinion of the peoples who owe allegiance to these Governments. The several nations would not disarm, but they might well begin to limit their armaments in accordance with the terms of a mutual agreement. The faces of mankind would be set toward a happier and more peaceful future, but neither Utopia nor the millennium would be reached at once.

XV

THE PART OF THE UNITED STATES IN THE ENFORCE-
MENT OF INTERNATIONAL LAW AND IN THE
ADMINISTRATION OF A NEW INTERNATIONAL
ORDER—THE MONROE DOCTRINE—A EUROPEAN
AND AN AMERICAN SPHERE OF ADMINISTRATIVE
ACTION—PREPARATION OF THE UNITED STATES
FOR INTERNATIONAL PARTICIPATION—NATIONAL
POLICY AND NATIONAL SERVICE

THE relation of the United States to the methods that will be adopted for the enforcement of international law and for the administration of an international order is a matter of highest concern not only to the people of the United States themselves but to the people of Europe as well. If, an international order having been established with the co-operation of the United States, the responsibility for the administration of that international order in Europe and in those parts of Asia and Africa that are politically dependent thereon, is a matter in which the United States will not directly concern itself, then it is important that this fact and its implications be clearly understood.

It is at this point that we come face to face with the traditional policy of the United States, built, it has always been believed, upon obedience to the injunction of Washington's Farewell Address and upon the declarations and policies that taken together constitute what is known as the Monroe Doctrine. It was this which the American delegates to the two Hague Conferences had in mind when they made the formal declaration of reservation that has already been quoted.

As a matter of pure theory it might readily be argued that, in looking to the future of the world's peace and comity, there is no reason why the United States should not unite on equal terms with the nations of Europe to assume international duties and responsibilities in all parts of the world. On the contrary, viewed theoretically, many reasons might be brought forward why such a new departure in policy on the part of the United States would be sound and judicious. Whatever may prove to be possible a century hence, it seems quite plain that as a practical matter the people of the United States could not now be induced to take any such novel and revolutionary steps. Their form of government is not well adjusted to possible action of this kind and their habits of thought would make any consistent and persistent co-operation of this sort probably out of the question, at least for the present and for some time to come.

It is, of course, true that the precise facts which Washington had in mind when he wrote his Farewell Address and those which Monroe had in mind when he sent his message of December 2, 1823, to the Congress, have long since changed. There is no longer any such thing as a European system of government which might be extended to this or any other continent. The spread of democratic ideas and principles has brought by far the larger number of European nations under their sway, and the love of liberty is just as strong in the breasts of those peoples as it is in the breasts of the people of the United States. Time is on the side of democracy. Those nations which still maintain barriers against it in their governmental forms are bound to give way with more or less good grace and in a shorter or a longer time. The gap which separates Europe and America is no longer one made by the difference between their political philosophies, for these have been steadily growing into closer accord. It is no longer one made by wide and tempestuous oceans crossed with danger and difficulty, for steam and electricity have united to make this distance almost negligible. The real gap is the one signified by the distinction between the names Old World and New World. This difference, which of course has its roots in history, may be in large part sentimental, but it is on that account none the less real and compelling. It was just this distinction which underlay the counsels of Washington. It would be foolish to treat those counsels as an injunction never to be modified or departed from, no matter what might be the changed conditions in the world, and it would be incorrect to read into them a severe and narrow meaning which they do not necessarily have; and yet it remains true that progress is more likely to be made by the American people through following those counsels and through modifying them in various ways as circumstances invite or compel than through departing from them entirely in an effort to strike out in new and hitherto untried paths.

The Monroe Doctrine is a national policy that has come to be widely recognized and in large part accepted by European nations. It is not a part of international law, but it might easily become so in the working out of an international order, responsibility for the administration of which will be divided into two spheres, one European, the other American. Before sending the message in which the Monroe Doctrine was announced, Monroe consulted Jefferson and received from him a well-known letter in which this striking passage occurs: "The question presented by letters you have sent me is the most momentous which has ever been offered to my contemplation since that of independence. That made us a nation; this sets our compass and points the course which we are to steer through the ocean of time opening on us. . . . Our first and fundamental maxim should be, never to entangle ourselves in the broils of Europe; our second, never to suffer Europe to intermeddle with Cis-Atlantic affairs." Shortly afterward Daniel Webster, who represented the opposite pole of political thought, speaking in his place in the House of Representatives, used these words of the Monroe Doctrine: "I will neither help to erase it or tear it out; nor shall it be, by any act of mine, blurred or blotted. It did honor to the sagacity of the Government, and I will not diminish that honor." Two generations later, in his message of December 17, 1895, to the Congress, President Cleveland described the Monroe Doctrine as intended to apply to every stage of our national life and to last while our republic endures.

While State papers give to the Monroe Doctrine more or less precise statement and significance, in the minds of the people as a whole it betokens rather a point of view and a general guiding principle of international policy. Even if it were desirable to attempt to change this national point of view and to alter this guiding principle of policy, it would be quite impracticable to do so. The Monroe Doctrine must be accepted as an elementary fact in attempting to arrive at any practical conclusion as to the participation of the United States in the administration of a new international order. So far as European territory and jurisdiction are concerned, the new international order will have to be administered by the European nations themselves. So far as American territory and jurisdiction are concerned, the new international order will have to be administered by the people of the United States in friendly concert with those of the other American republics.

The formal erection of these two separate jurisdictions need not in the least weaken the position or the influence of the United States in the counsels and semi-legislative acts which will lay the basis for a durable peace, and out of which the new international order will grow. Neither should it be held to deprive the people of the United States of the opportunity and the right to give expression to their feelings and convictions when questions of law and justice, of right and wrong, are raised as between nations in any part of the world. It simply means that for the reasons stated and on the grounds given the direct responsibility of the Government of the United States for the enforcement of the new international order will be limited to the American continents and to territory belonging to some one of the American republics.

For participation in this task of international counsel and of better international administration the people of the United States must prepare themselves. They must come to understand, while the largest measure of local self-government is vital to the continued existence and effective working of our domestic institutions, that when the nation acts in foreign policy it must act as a unit and its action must be everywhere upheld. A wrong step in domestic legislation can be corrected with no damage to any one but ourselves. A wrong step in foreign policy, however, can never be corrected, for it affects not only ourselves but the opinion which others have of us. The present German Emperor is reported to have said on one occasion that he did not see how his Government could ever make another treaty with the United States, because, under our constitutional law, treaty provisions, so far as they were municipal law in the United States, might be

and frequently were modified or repealed by a subsequent act of Congress without any formal notice
to the other high contracting party. It is, of course,
well known that the treaty-making power of the
United States bristles with difficult and delicate
questions, and it must be conceded that if the United
States is to become an effective international influence in support of the ideas and principles upon
which its own Government and polity are based, and
if it is to lend useful aid in securing and maintaining a durable peace, it must first set its own house
in order. It must have a care to make no international agreements and to assume no international
responsibilities which it will not keep and bear to the
full, at whatever cost to itself. Having made such
engagements they must be scrupulously observed.
To bring this to pass means that the treaty-making
power must not march far in advance of supporting
public opinion and that the whole power of the Government must be available to enforce the terms of a
treaty once entered into.

These questions of constitutional law and of political policy are bound up with questions affecting the
military and naval systems of the United States.
Competition in armaments is the worst possible
form of international rivalry; but to take a seat at
an international council table in the present state of
world public opinion and world policy without some
effective means of representing a nation's purpose
is to reduce such participation to mere futile debate.
The other liberty-loving nations would be quite

justified in asking two questions of the representatives of the United States: first, what are the policies which you believe to be just and practicable as part of a new international order; and, second, what contribution can you and will you make to the support of that international order if you join with us in bringing it into being? It is, perhaps, by coming face to face with these searching questions that the people of the United States will most quickly be brought to realize what new domestic policies they must enter upon in order to prepare themselves for international participation. The spirit of international and of national devotion which time and time again has triumphed over provincialism, local interest, and selfishness must be appealed to once more. National service can no longer remain an empty phrase, but must be given life and meaning and universal application. As the spirit and principles of democracy require that there be the widest possible participation in the formulation of public policy, so this spirit and these principles require that there shall be the widest possible participation in the nation's service, and, if need be, in its defense. An army of hired soldiers as the chief dependence of a democratic people is as much of an anachronism as an army of hired voters would be. The country's system of public education must be taken in strong hand, purged of much of its sentimentality and weak and futile philosophizing, and made more and more a genuine preparation of American youth for intelligent and helpful participation in American life.

Outside of and beyond the public educational system of the nation there should be established without delay a system of universal training for national service and, should it ever be needed, for national defense. Such a policy is the antithesis of militarism; it is democracy conscious and mindful of its duties and responsibilities as well as of its rights.

The people of the United States will never become an important agency in the development of helpful world policies unless they first take those steps that both entitle and enable them genuinely to participate in such a task. Every belligerent nation is receiving at the hands of this war the severest possible course of instruction and discipline. Every important belligerent nation will emerge from this war a generation or perhaps a century in advance of the United States in all that pertains to national service, to national sacrifice, and to that strengthening of character which comes not from talking about ideals but from actively supporting them in the most fiery of contests. It is for the people of the United States to find ways and means of learning the lessons of the war without having to pay the awful cost in life and treasure which military participation in it involves. Their future place in the world's history, the regard which other nations will have for them, and their own more fortunate and just development all depend upon the way in which these searching problems are solved. It deprives a nation's voice of half its force if it protests against cruelty and oppression and injustice abroad while there are cruelty and oppression and injustice at home. The war has forced all these considerations upon Great Britain and France and Germany and Russia and the rest, and they are dealing with them each in its own way. The war has also forced these considerations upon the people of the United States. How are they going to deal with them? Will they merely wish to have a durable peace, or will they so act at home and abroad as to help to insure a durable peace?

XVI

CONCLUSION—QUESTIONS FOR THE FUTURE—THE ESSENTIALS OF A DURABLE PEACE

THE ground proposed to be covered in these discussions has now been traversed. Starting with the assumptions that the principles and policies for which the Allies are contending must prevail if the war is to be followed by a durable peace, and that the progress of military operations thus far has made it plain that Germany and the Powers associated with her cannot possibly win the war but must in all probability shortly give way before the military and economic superiority of the Allies, an effort was first made to find a possible point of departure for the consideration of the basis of a durable peace. This appeared to be provided by certain recent statements of Viscount Grey and Chancellor von Bethmann-Hollweg as to the objects for which the Allies and the Germanic Powers, respectively, are contending. A comparison of these statements led to a discussion of what is meant by the rights of nations, great and small, and of what is involved in providing them with a satisfactory guarantee for their security, including the open door policy in international trade. An examination of the meaning of the phrase "freedom of the seas" followed, and then a discussion of the part played by France and by Russia in the war, and of the specific acts and policies which would probably be asked for by them as conditions of a durable peace. It next became necessary to analyze what is meant by Prussian militarism, which it is a chief aim of the Allies to destroy. So much being premised, there followed an examination of the progress heretofore made in the establishment of an international order, and this was followed by specific suggestions for the development and strengthening of that international order in ways and for the purposes that have been set forth in detail. It was natural to examine next, with some particularity, the possible and the probable attitude of the people of the United States toward such an international order, toward its administration, and toward the future enforcement of international law. As a corollary to the examination of these points, some suggestions were offered as to the lessons of this war for the people of the United States in matters of their own domestic policy.

In this survey many matters, some of them highly important, have been left on one side. There is, for example, the question as to the best disposition, in the interest of a durable peace, of the colonial possessions that were held by Germany at the outbreak of the war. This naturally raises questions as to the future policy of the civilized nations toward the whole subject of colonization and the assumption of sovereignty over new territory. Then there is the Far East, with its special problems. At the moment this is an area in which both the European nations and the United States participate, after a fashion, in the carrying out of various important policies of an international character. Whether it would be best to look forward to a continuance, for some time at least, of this general relationship, or whether it would be better to institute in the Far East a third administrative area for the carrying on of an international order and the enforcement of international law, with chief responsibility in the hands of Japan, that nation, operating under a sort of Asiatic Monroe Doctrine, is well worth considering.

Important questions suggest themselves as to the domestic policy of various peoples toward races and religions represented in the populations dependent upon them, which frequently give rise to international unrest and international friction. Instances of this sort are the Armenians in Turkey, the Finns in Russia, the Serbians in Austria, and the Jews in both Russia and Rumania. Not all of these vexed questions will be answered within the lifetime of any one now living; but if certain principles of national and international conduct are kept clearly in view, and if an international order is erected on those principles as a foundation and a true International Court of Justice established, then a possible way will have been provided for the calm consideration and judicial examination of even such perplexing questions as these.

Finally, there is the whole question of disarmament, or rather the limitation of armaments, the presentation of which by the Tsar was the formal reason for the calling of the first Hague Conference. This same question, it must be remembered, was considered by the British representatives at the second Hague Conference to have a bearing on the so-called freedom of the seas, and particularly on the exemption of private property, not contraband, from capture. Even if what appears to be a durable peace is the outcome of the present war, it is plain that the world will have left enough hard problems of an international character to occupy it, even without war, for generations to come.

The deep underlying causes of the present war must be understood and taken into full consideration in any discussion of a durable peace that is to have practical value. By this is not meant the narrow question of the precise sequence of events from July 23 to August 1, 1914, or the weight to be attached to any given act or word of any particular Government at that hectic time. All these matters, as was said at the outset of these discussions, are for the time at least of merely historical interest. Some day the dispassionate writer of history will set out an account of them which will govern the belief of the generations that are to come; but this is after all a minor matter. The real underlying cause of the war was an irrepressible conflict between two views and ideals of national development and of civilization. As has already been explained, the militaristic policy of Prussia, extended for the time being over all Germany and Germany's allies, represents and gives voice to an old and dying order. Perhaps that militaristic policy was at one time necessary to the development not only of Prussia and of Germany but of the world at large; but if so, it has long since served its proper purpose and must now give way to the wiser, more humane, and more advanced philosophy of national and international life, for which the Allies, despite all their superficial differences, are contending with an amazing singleness of purpose.

To conquer the militaristic ideal, as represented for the moment by Prussian policy, will not be enough to insure a durable peace. The spirit and the point of view which manifest themselves in militarism, in the subordination of civil to military authority and policy, and in the setting of right below might, must be driven out of the hearts and minds of men. It will not be enough to drive them out of the hearts and minds of Prussians and Germans; they must be driven out of the hearts and minds of those Englishmen, those Frenchmen, those Russians, those Americans, and those Japanese in which they may have found lodgment. This can take place only if the minds and purposes of men are controlled by something that is more powerful than militarism because it is more moral and more helpful to mankind. In other words, the basis of sound international policy will be found in sound domestic policy, and in sympathy with equally sound domestic policies in other lands. As nations come more and more to see that their greatness consists in doing justice and securing happiness at home rather than in extending their physical power over their neighbors and in forcing their trade by undue and unfair grants of privilege, the peaceful area of the world will rapidly widen.

The institutions which the new international order that has here been proposed and outlined will erect, should be and doubtless will be of the greatest value in educating the mind of the world toward healthier and wiser international relationships, but those institutions cannot do the work alone. They must have behind them the driving force of a purpose to keep the peace, of a desire to execute in spirit as well as in letter international engagements, and also a curbing of those cruder and more brutal forms of patriotism which manifest themselves by doing injustice and wrong to others. If it be said that such a development would mean the breaking down of nations and of nationalism as a force in the world, the answer is that it will do nothing of the sort. The individual human being whose acts are controlled by an overmastering sense of duty is not less of a person, but more, than the individual human being whose acts are controlled by sheer selfishness. What is true of men in this regard is true also of nations. A nation, like an individual, will become greater as it cherishes a high ideal and does service and helpful acts to its neighbors whether great or small, and as it co-operates with them in working toward a common end. If this be pronounced Utopian, then Utopia is the goal for which every moral person in the world is laboring.

Though to be defeated in this war, the German people will, on that very account, have a still more important part to play in civilization than has yet fallen to their lot. They have, it is complained, come late into the world, and found the choice places already possessed by others. But the choice places in political development, in administrative competence, in uplifting and making comfortable the great mass of the population, in developing literature and science and art, and in finding new ways to express the joy and satisfaction of living, are always open to the possession of any one qualified to enter into them. The sense of duty has taken a strong hold of the German people ever since Fichte's time. It has mightily increased the excellence of their excellences and it has greatly magnified the seriousness of their defects. Should this war prove to be a burning up of the most powerful remnants of militarism that yet remain in the world, it will have done the German people the greatest possible service. One hundred and twenty millions of eager, active, purposeful men, living in the temperate zone and having a long tradition of heroic endeavor, cannot be reduced to nothingness by any power but their own. Stripped of the militaristic purpose and brought into harmony with the other great peoples of the world, the Germans would, it may safely be predicted, enter upon a new period of usefulness and achievement that would make the history of the last hundred years seem paltry by comparison. What Frederick William III so finely said when the humiliation of

Jena was still fresh may well be repeated one hundred and ten years afterward.

In conclusion, then, a durable peace depends upon the victory of the Allies in the present war and upon the establishment in public policy of the principles for which they are contending. It depends upon a withholding of all acts of vengeance and reprisal, and the just and statesmanlike application to each specific problem that arises for settlement of the principles for which the war is being fought. It depends upon the establishment of an international order and of those international institutions that have been here sketched in outline. It depends upon a spirit of devotion to that order and to those institutions, as well as upon a fixed purpose to uphold and to defend them. It depends upon domestic policies of justice and helpfulness, and the curbing of arrogance, greed, and privilege, so far as it is within the power of government to do so. It depends upon the exaltation of the idea of justice, not only as between men within a nation, but as between nations themselves; for durable peace is a by-product of justice. When these things are accomplished there will be every prospect of a durable peace because the essential prerequisite will have been provided—the Will to Peace.

APPENDIX

I

HALL CAINE TO COSMOS

(Cable to *The New York Times*)

LONDON, November 25, 1916.

To Cosmos:

The New York Times has done me, with others, the honor of asking me to reply to your plea for immediate peace. I recognize in your opinions and in your method of presenting them a marked resemblance to the opinions and methods of certain distinguished and honored Englishmen, but, assuming that you are an American, I begin by saying that your whole argument, so far as it has been made known to us on this side of the ocean, labors under the disadvantage of your aloofness from the emotions excited by the war. We have it on ancient authority that the lookers-on see most of the game; but it will not be denied that the players feel most of it, and we think it is necessary to feel as well as to see this war in order to know which is the moment most favorable for a discussion of peace.

I think you have failed to see that the first condition of such a discussion is not the military position of the belligerents but their spiritual temper. You say that the similarity of the recent utterances of Viscount Grey and Herr von Bethmann Hollweg gives hope of a formula that would satisfy both, but we think the peace speech of the German Chancellor was inspired by the idea of peace with German victory behind it, and we are not surprised that the German people should think that the so-called peace speech of the British Foreign Secretary was inspired by a corresponding idea of peace with a victory for the Allies behind it. Not until one or the other of these ministers approaches the subject without the thought of victory, or with the idea of submission, or the theory of a drawn war can conditions come to that point which is favorable to a discussion of peace. We see no sign whatever of that condition either in England or Germany at the present moment.

CAUSE OF WAR STILL AN ISSUE

We gather that you think it is useless to concern ourselves now with any question of the causes of the war. We, on the contrary, think that this is not only necessary, but inevitable, to any hopeful consideration of peace. We think the war had its origin in a plot; that this plot found its climax in the Austrian ultimatum to Serbia; that Serbia could only have accepted that ultimatum by ceasing to be a nation; that the German Ambassador at Vienna certainly, and the Kaiser probably, knew and approved of the terms of the ultimatum before it was despatched; that the deliberate object of the ultimatum was to break the peace of Europe in the interests of Germany's designs; that Germany regarded the war, not merely as a necessary evil, but as a laudable means of obtaining dominion, and that the subjugation of Serbia and the violation of Belgium were the logical outcome of this false and wicked policy. We see no evidence that Germany has repented of that plot, and no prospect of a lasting and authentic peace until she does repent of it or suffer for not doing so.

We also gather that you think that, inasmuch as it is impossible at this moment to discuss the motives of the belligerents, it ought to be sufficient for us to recognize that, equally with ourselves, Germany believes she is in the right. But that Germany believes she is in the right makes her, in our view, all the more wrong, and a discussion of terms of peace all the more impossible. Only when she realizes that she is in the wrong can we approach a discussion of a peace that will be permanent, because based not merely on military necessities but on a practical recognition of the precepts of moral law. Of such a realization we see no sign in Germany at present.

You think that the time has come for a consideration of

peace because Germany must now know that she cannot win the war, and because the Allies must see that they can only win at a cost that would be scarcely less disastrous than defeat; but we think this is a condition that is less than half-way toward peace. Only when Germany sees she must certainly lose the war, or when the Allies feel that the worst disasters which may result from going on with it will not be atoned for by the triumph of the principles they are fighting for can the favorable moment come for a peace that will be founded merely on calculations of loss or gain. We see no evidence whatever that the belligerents are yet willing to accept these conclusions.

Wicked Waste in Ending War Now

We gather that you think that because the war has gone on so long without producing any results except immeasurable misery it should stop, having failed in whatever object the belligerents expected from it; but it is just because the war has thus far produced no definite military results that we think it cannot stop. We think that to end the war now, after so much suffering and sacrifice, by any form of inconclusive peace, which would prove and establish nothing, would be waste—wanton, wicked, irretrievable, inexcusable, blind, and blinding waste such as we dare not for one moment contemplate. We think such a peace would be treason to the dead, disloyalty to the living, an assault on the authority of government, an open appeal to the lawlessness of anarchy, a deliberate outrage on the principles of patriotism, and even on the sacred precepts of religion.

You think the time favorable for a discussion of peace, because the Allies, though they may well win, cannot want, and would not, probably, be able utterly to crush their enemies. But though such of us as know history and take a human view of war and its probable results have never hoped for or dreamed of the extermination of Germany as an empire, we have, indeed, hoped for and dreamed of the destruction of the German political ideal which is based, as we see it, on the idea that civilization, culture, and the general welfare of the human family are secured by the dominion and tyranny of the sword, with its inevitable consequences of the violation of the liberties of little nations and the general Germanizing of the world. After two and a half years of war we see no sign yet that Germany has parted company with this ideal and therefore no indication of a peace that could be built on Christian principles of the equal rights of all peoples.

You think that to prolong the war at a cost of more and worse suffering would lead to such exacerbation of the feelings of the belligerents as would be deleterious to the future peace of Europe. We think, on the contrary, that to end it at this inconclusive stage, when neither side can be said to have reached a military conclusion, would be the surest way to create other wars, by giving time for recuperation and a renewal of hostilities which neither of the belligerents has repented of or seen the futility of pursuing.

You think that though Germany may have been the sinister aggressor she has learned her lesson and that if peace comes now she may be relied upon to do her best to prevent more wars. We think, on the other hand, that the only lesson Germany has yet learned is a military lesson, the lesson that has come of setting too low a value on the power, courage, and resources of her enemies, and that the only safeguard of enduring peace is that she should also learn the moral lesson that comes of seeing the uselessness of war as a means toward human welfare. Of that lesson Germany, so far as we can see, has yet learned nothing.

WHY THE WAR MUST GO ON

You think, so far as I can judge, that if peace came now both belligerents would recognize the folly of war as a means of settling international disputes, and so having jointly learned their lesson would strive together to avoid its recurrence.

We think, on the contrary, that such recognition could only come to both at once after complete exhaustion, and then the only value of the lesson would be to the rest of the world—America, for example, which surely cannot need it. It is probably true that a full sense of the futility and foolishness of war will come to the world only out of the spectacle of the great part of it ruined, vanquished, and laid waste; but even this does not shake our feeling that worse than the utmost ruin that can be wrought by war, terrible and awful as that may be, is the spiritual enslavement that may be prevented by it. God forbid that the very least of us against any hopeful plea for peace should say one word that would prolong the horrors of war, but we of the allied nations hate war with so deep a hatred that the hope of ending it once for all inspires us to carry it on. It is just because our hearts are bleeding from the frightful sacrifices we are now making day by day in the best of our blood and brain that we feel, terribly and cruelly hard as it is to say it, that they must continue to bleed. Nor do we think that these impulses conflict either with the best interests of civilization or with our faith.

We are acutely and most painfully conscious that in struggling for what we believe with all our souls to be right we have been compelled to submit the issue of our cause to a power which has in itself nothing to do with right. We know that our religion teaches us that Christ pronounced anathema on war, and that as soon as Christianity shall have established its ascendency war will cease; but we also know and have lately been made most bitterly to feel that war is sometimes necessary to keep the worst elements of human nature in check, that an appeal to might may be the last resources of right, and therefore it is right to fight and to continue to fight for a righteous cause. On this foundation we of the allied nations, with extreme reluctance, in August, 1914, built our belief in the necessity of entering into the present conflict.

And what would be the result now if after two and a

half years of a war which has convulsed Europe, sweeping armies of men into innumerable graves and bringing misery to millions of women and children, we were to make peace with an unrepentant enemy on the grounds of expediency alone? We think there would be only one result, the complete breakdown in Europe of all moral law in the government of nations and all faith in the divine rule of the world.

CONFIDENCE IN THE UNITED STATES

We are profoundly grateful to the United States for the watchful eye it has always kept and is still keeping on the prospects of peace, and we sleep with more security from a certainty that the one world empire which remains outside this maelstrom of devastating forces will step in with proposals to end the war the instant it becomes right and possible to do so.

Meantime we rest content with the part America is now taking and will, we trust, continue to take. That part is the part of the friend and champion, not of either belligerent, but of humanity. In our view it has been a long step forward from the rigid and frozen neutrality which America imposed on her people at the beginning of war to the recent warm-blooded declaration of her President that henceforward neutrality is impossible to a great nation in any conflict which affects the welfare of a vast part of the human family.

That is not a new doctrine, but it is a great doctrine. It was the doctrine whereon the mighty Englishman, Oliver Cromwell, made England not only the most powerful but the most honored among the nations of the world, and in the midst of the revivals of methods of warfare which seem to us to be destitute of all distinction between right and wrong, and to deserve no other names than murder and slavery, we shall be satisfied if America should continue to stand steadfastly for the high principle, on whichever side assailed, that the laws of humanity, which are immutable, shall not be outraged.   That of itself will help to keep the spirit of justice alive in the world and go far toward bringing nearer the day of peace.

HALL CAINE.

II

COSMOS TO HALL CAINE

November 27, 1916.

To Hall Caine:

By the courtesy of *The New York Times* I am able to make immediate reply to your cabled letter dated November 25. You have quite misunderstood the purpose of my discussions. This misunderstanding is doubtless due to the imperfect or partial form in which they have reached you.   It may be due in part to the fact that, at the moment of their publication, there were made both in this country and elsewhere a number of expressions of opinion regarding the termination of the war with which my discussions may have been quite unjustifiably associated.   The misunderstanding may be due in part to the caption under which they were printed.

I make no plea for immediate peace.   On the contrary, I entirely dissociate myself from those persons and those movements which would urge, on humanitarian grounds, an immediate peace, even at the cost of the great objects of the war.   Until those objects are gained and, having been gained, are secured for the future, this war cannot end in anything that would deserve the name of peace.   Under such circumstances the result would be at best a new era of competitive armaments and a new and desperate struggle, by the use of every means known to man, to gain a position of advantage from which to carry on another and equally terrible contest.

The starting-point of my discussions, assuming the certain defeat of Germany and her allies, is the belief that the time has come to consider whether the war may not be ended in the not distant future by an international agreement in which the United States shall participate. With a view to securing a basis for the discussion of such an international agreement certain definite proposals are being brought forward and examined in my contributions to *The New York Times*. It would be most helpful if, when these specific proposals have been read in full and carefully considered, it might then be pointed out how far, if at all, they may be made to serve as the basis of a future international agreement whose aim shall be to do everything that is humanly possible to protect civilization against a recurrence of the present calamity.

You are mistaken, too, in assuming that these articles have been written under the disadvantage of aloofness from the emotions excited by the war. While an effort has been made to keep any expression of these emotions from appearing in the discussions, this has been a difficult task because of the depth of the writer's feelings. No one to whom the cause of the Allies in this war does not make a profound emotional appeal is likely to be at all able to contribute to a discussion of the terms of a durable peace.

COSMOS.

III

HALL CAINE TO COSMOS

(Cable to *The New York Times*)

LONDON, November 29, 1916.

To Cosmos:

By courtesy of *The New York Times* I have read your letter cabled on Monday, and I hasten to say that hardly anything could be less like the general purport of your articles, as made known to us by the digest published on this side of the ocean. That digest represented them as a peace kite, flown possibly in German interests, or at least capable of being turned to Germany's account. But my letter was not inspired by that injurious interpretation. On the contrary, it was suggested by regret that such language should be employed by a responsible organ of British opinion about a writer who was obviously sincere and in relation to a journal, *The New York Times*, which has published some of the most enlightening, searching, deeply felt and sympathetic articles that have appeared in any country during the period of the war.

My letter was also prompted by a desire to make recognition of the obvious fact that the United States could only be inspired by the noblest motives of humanity—against the manifest opposition of material interests—in initiating a propaganda in favor of peace.

Therefore I did my best to answer you on the high ground of moral law, not of military opportunity or necessity, frequently quoting the precise terms attributed to you and drawing no inferences from your argument except such as seemed to be fair to the general trend of it. In doing this I think I represented the spirit of our people, who are not ungrateful to America for what she is doing, and would certainly not presume to banish the word "peace" from the vocabulary of the greatest of neutral nations, however little they may desire to use it themselves.

But if you feel that you have cause for complaint in the language sometimes held toward America in this country, I ask you to put yourself in our place. It may be true that the Junkers are not all in Germany, that the Huns are not all in Prussia, that boastful and overbearing threats are used here as well as beyond the Rhine, and that in the midst of the immeasurable suffering that has been created by the war the loudest clamor against proposals for peace may in this country, as in the countries of our enemies, come from the warlike pulpits, heroic sofas, and invincible armchairs; but that is by no means the whole story.

Our people are a proud, brave, high-spirited race, unaccustomed to defeat and unwilling to bear the shame of it. In times past we have known the full bitterness of dark and threatening hours. Less than three centuries ago, after a period of world supremacy, we saw the Dutch fleet riding triumphantly in the Thames. Less than two centuries ago, on the eve of our greatest victories, we saw our forces broken on land and sea.

But our national spirit has never been broken. We have never yet submitted to a disgraceful peace, and now, when we are, as we believe, the victim of a cruel and cowardly plot, when we are suffering with our allies and with some of the neutral nations, not excluding America, from every imaginable horror of treacherous warfare which inhumanity can devise or barbarity execute, we feel that it is not for us to prate about peace until it is near, and we know it to be right.

Let our enemies squeal for it, whether in bravado or fear. It is not in the spirit of our people to do so, whatever price we have to pay for our silence. That is the first trait of our national character, and not to know it is not to know our Britain—what it is and what it has gone through.

Some of us who have it for our duty to speak to our people through great newspapers from day to day or week to week have been made acutely conscious of this undying national characteristic. There are subjects we cannot discuss because our people do not admit that they come within the realm of question. There are eventualities we cannot contemplate because they are not believed to be within the region of possibilities, and above all such subjects and eventualities is the subject and eventuality of a peace that shall be premature and therefore dishonoring and dangerous. On that question, in spite of all our sufferings, past, present, and to come, the soul of our Empire is on fire. Hence the impatience and even suspicion with which some of the so-called peace talk of America has been received in this country, and hence, too, the misconception which, as your letter shows, sometimes prevails as to the scope and aim of it.

With the general trend of your letter, as cabled to me, I find myself in complete agreement. That when the war has been righteously ended (God grant it may be soon!) an effort ought to be made to establish an international agreement whose aim would be to protect civilization against the recurrence of such another calamity is a proposition that will commend itself to the vast majority of my countrymen, and it will seem to us to be fit and right that America should take the lead in this high enterprise as the one great nation whose power would command authority throughout the world, and whose hands are clean of the present crime.

But in joining your league of peace we should have no illusions. We should not necessarily think that we were promoting the peace principles of the Founder of our faith. Those principles, as most of us understand them, are based on the cry that violence in whatever form employed produces violence, and that the only way to establish the rule of moral law is not to resist evil.

But we see that that doctrine may make martyrs and religions, not nations, and that your international league of peace would have to be founded on force. Like a civil government, it would depend in the final resort on the power behind it, and therefore be liable to deadlocks and breakdowns and some of the lesser dangers of present conditions.

On the other hand, we recognize the difference that the force behind your league of peace would be a world force, not a national force. That difference would be fundamental. It would give us reason to hope that moral law would be allowed to operate in international disputes, and therefore an ultimatum like that of Austria to Serbia would be impossible; that the rights of little nations would be considered apart from the power to enforce them, and therefore the violations of Belgium and the enslavement of her people would be unthinkable, and, above all, that such a world war as we are in the midst of, involving incalculable sufferings to millions, would never again be undertaken after a few delirious days of intoxicating diplomacy, conducted in secret by a handful of men who are not all distinguished for intelligence or above the suspicion of unworthy motives.

If America in due time can bring to pass a coalition like that, it will have rendered a service to humanity such as the world has hardly yet dared to hope for. So blessed a consummation would almost reconcile us to the immeasurable misery of the present frightful conflict by making us feel that for this reason God permitted it that, as once by flood so now by fire, the world might be purged of the worst of its impurities; that He has allowed nothing to be wasted, no suffering, no sacrifice; and that through the grandeur as well as the sorrow of the time He has given to his stricken world a glorious resurrection. God grant it!

HALL CAINE.

IV

COSMOS TO HIS CRITICS

December 1, 1916.

To the Editor of The New York Times:

To a number of letters that have reached me through you, written either in criticism or in commendation of my discussions now appearing in *The Times* as to the basis of that durable peace which all nations, whether belligerent or neutral, profess to desire, I should like to make brief acknowledgment and reply.

Let me repeat once more that these discussions presuppose the military and economic victory of the Allies over the Central Powers and the continuance of the war until it appears to be certain that an international agreement can be formulated which will, first, accomplish and make secure the ends for which the Allies are prosecuting the war, and, second, make every provision that is humanly possible against the outbreak of a similar international struggle in the future.

These discussions are addressed primarily to Americans, in the hope that public opinion in the United States may be led to inform itself specifically and in detail as to the precise ends of the war and as to the ways and means of accomplishing and making secure those ends when terms of peace are drawn up. The United States is a neutral participant in this war and is directly and profoundly interested in the outcome, not only on the field of battle but in the realm of political ideas and policies. It was hoped, of course, that these discussions would be, as they are being, followed in Europe, in order that to some extent at least the mind of the United States and the mind of Europe might be assisted to meet, at least in some degree, in regard to the vital issues under examination.

Let me repeat once more that these discussions have not been written and printed as part of any pro-German propaganda for an immediate peace, and that they have no connection, direct or indirect, with any organization or movement in this or other countries speedily to end the war on the basis of a drawn military battle. It is a mere coincidence, and not a fortunate one, that these discussions have been printed at a time when such organizations and movements are prominently in the public eye.

Let me suggest also that it would be more satisfactory and also more flattering if my correspondents would take the pains to read these discussions before either criticising or commending them.

Cosmos.

V

THE ARTICLES OF COSMOS

From *The New York Times*, December 18

In the series of articles contributed by Cosmos to the columns of *The Times*, the sixteenth and concluding article appearing this morning, we have heard the voice of reason amid the clash of arms. The conditions upon which a lasting peace must be based after the end of the war have been his theme. A sound understanding of the rivalry of interests, the political maladjustments and the false ideals out of which the war grew was his qualification, justice and the deep conviction that out of this war must come measures of assurance against future wars have guided him to his conclusions. The articles of Cosmos have called forth some criticism, even more they have stimulated discussion. They are a comprehensive prevision of the readjustments after the war that are essential to enduring peace.

In the opening sentence of his ninth article the writer of these contributions restated the conditions which, in his judgment, must be the basis of peace if it is to be lasting:

"The ground that has now been traversed includes the outline of a settlement of the issues of the war that would insure the free national development of every state whether great or small, the policy of the open door in international trade, the exemption of private property at sea, other than contraband, from capture or destruction, and that would restore Alsace-Lorraine to France as well as make Russia mistress of the Dardanelles and the Bosporus."

There remains that other purpose of the war of which Mr. Asquith said that Great Britain would never sheathe the sword, not lightly drawn, until it had been accomplished, the complete and final destruction of Prussian militarism, that "state of the Prussian mind," as Cosmos calls it, that has made Germany a militaristic nation. There remains, too, reparation to Belgium by Germany, to Serbia by Austria.

The enduring safeguards against war which nations must erect, the league of all to secure peace for all, provision for commissions of inquiry to examine causes of difference, and an International Court of Justice have been discussed in the concluding articles of the series with a remarkable breadth of view and a clear comprehension both of what is desired and of the difficulties that lie in the way. Particularly illuminating is the discussion of the nature of the measures by which sanction and enforcement are to be given to agreements among nations, which must be made binding if any good thing is to come of them, and of the part the United States, in view of its Monroe Doctrine and its traditional detachment from European politics, may safely and properly take upon itself. And there are words of admonition addressed to our people and to our States, warnings of what must follow their failure to come to a due sense of national duty and national service, of which it will be well for all Americans to take heed.

In inviting these contributions from Cosmos and in publishing them, *The Times* feels that it has performed a service of which the value will become strikingly evident when, after the war, the conditions of peace, in all their variety, consequences, and projections, come to the test of practical discussion. Cosmos has brought into view not merely terms and conditions but fundamental principles.

INDEX OF PROPER NAMES